DEDICATION

This book is dedicated to
Maria and Jozef Pawlukiewicz, my parents.
It is not a work of fiction, but a factual account
portraying the lives of two ordinary individuals
whose courage, valor, and faith preserved
them during an atrocious time in our
world's history and in their lives.

Tears of Hope

A Story of Love, Hope and Survival
during Soviet Imprisonment

Irena M. Rozycki

By Irena Maria Rozycki

Comments: polroz@aol.com

ISBN: 978-1-941069-45-5

Cover Design: OBD

Prose Press
Pawleys Island
South Carolina 29585
prosencons@live.com

ACKNOWLEDGEMENT

There are numerous people who were a part of my life and who encouraged me to write this book. Therefore, they need to know that my gratitude is immense.

To John, my husband of over forty years, I am grateful for your love and support in not only completing this book, but for believing in my pursuit of an education and career while caring for my family.

To my daughters, Elizabeth, Mary-Jean, Alicia, and Veronica who are all unique and special women without whom I could not have succeeded in this endeavor. This is for you and your families, so that you can continue to appreciate Babcia and Dziadzia.

To Veronica, special thanks for typing my hand-written book onto a disc (since my computer skills are nil) and for her numerous editorial comments.

To Olivia, Julia, Sabrina, Sophia, Soraya, and Savanna – my lovely and intelligent granddaughters. This book was written for you so that you could get to know your great-grandparents and realize that because of their struggles, your grandmother and grandfather, both immigrants to America, worked very hard so that your parents could eventually provide a wonderful life for all of you.

To Julia and Olivia, my oldest granddaughters, for reading my manuscript and commenting in an intelligent, thoughtful manner, special thanks and lots of hugs.

To my friend and mentor, Jeffrey Hollman, an author, playwright, and artist, who motivated me and believed in my ability to get this book written, my sincere and lasting gratitude. Special thanks for editing the manuscript and adding much needed comments.

To Sharon Brown, Ed. D., a wonderful new friend in Myrtle Beach, and also a fellow educator, for accepting the task of editing this book and offering invaluable suggestions. Thank you many times over – you are an angel for all the advice you've provided.

To the Social Studies teachers at Half Hollow Hills High School East who invited me into their classes, especially Mrs. Cynthia Yantz-Cullen, an exceptional teacher of the Holocaust course, for requesting that I relate this unknown portion of World War II history. Ms. Joanne Rubin deserves thanks for inviting me to her class to teach about the Soviet Holocaust and for videotaping my lesson. Ms. Elizabeth Desmond is worthy of special thanks for allowing me to relate my parents' experiences in her English classes when she was teaching <u>One Day in the Life of Ivan Denisovich</u> (a book which portrayed my father's prison existence so clearly).

I am also especially grateful to my friend from Queen of the Rosary Academy days to the present, Joan Lundin, for her belief in me and for her "constant as the Northern star" support. Thank you for your many years of friendship – love you Joanie !

To my nephews Steven, and of course Trish, and Andrew Nauss, who knew I was working on this project and cheered me on as I worked to complete this task, I am forever thankful.

Much gratitude also to my former students from Holy Family High School, Plainedge High School, and Half Hollow Hills High School East, and past colleagues and innumerable friends from Long Island and Myrtle Beach, who encouraged me to complete this history of my parents' lives. Thank you everyone for my fifteen minutes of fame!

Foreword

Children's memories of their parents are often skewed for a variety of reasons, often because they do not want to listen to their mother's or father's life experiences. Fortunately, I was not such a child. I paid attention to my parents' story from the time I was about four until they both passed. I was attentive as they told and retold their horrors of war to friends and family. Sometimes, I felt as if I were present during every segment of their lives. I appreciated everything they went through and was proud of how courageous and brave they were, despite the adversities they endured. It amazed me that they never wavered in their faith in God. I remember seeing my father praying the Rosary often and my mother watching daily Mass on television when she could not attend church due to her health. Their home, as anyone who visited could attest, housed numerous religious paintings, statues, and icons. Their belief in the power of God helped them survive World War II and Soviet slave labor camps.

It wasn't until after I retired that I decided that their story had to be told. Their grandchildren and great-grandchildren needed to know the history of their family. Portions of Maria and Jozef's lives were harrowing, but their love for each other and their children propelled them toward survival. Like all human beings they were not perfect; nevertheless, they loved one another, God, their family, and their adopted country, perfectly.

"Hope" is the thing with feathers -
That perches in the soul -
And sings the tune without the words -
And never stops - at all.

By Emily Dickinson

Pre-World War II
Poland – 1920's

Chapter One

Jozefa straightened her back as she gazed at the acres of land before her. It was a lovely farm that she and her husband, Pawel, owned. Forests, farmland, grazing meadows, and lakes were visible as far as her eyes could see across the horizon. She loved this area of Poland and was proud of what she and Pawel had achieved up to this point in their lives. Her moment of solitude was interrupted when her daughter, Maria, asked her pensive mother an unusual question.

"Mother, where is Russia?"

"Why do you ask, my child?"

Maria looked musingly into the horizon before answering her mother. "I don't know, but all my life I've wondered?" Jozefa laughed at her blue-eyed daughter who had just turned ten in March of 1924.

"For such a young girl, you ask questions that your poor mother truly can't answer because I really don't know myself. But one of my brothers went there many years ago to fight in the Czar's war and never returned.

I never knew if he died in a battle or married a Russian woman and settled there. But that was long ago child and I don't even remember what he looked like. And as for Russia, all I know is that it's to the east of our home and very, very far away. People in our village say it's as far as 'where the devil says good night.' Now let's get back to getting these potatoes harvested before your father gets in from the other fields."

Maria watched her mother's bent-body harvesting the crop as she tagged along pulling the burlap sacks as best as she could. She was only ten, but her body was beginning to gather strength as her slim arms began to develop the muscles needed for her life as a farmer's wife in not too many years to come. But thoughts of Russia remained fertile in her mind. She heard Russia discussed by her father and his friends at one time or another in her young life since Zoltuny, the village of her birth, was not such a great distance from Russia's border as her mother envisioned. So the seed of curiosity had been planted in this young girl's inquisitive mind and, unbeknownst to her at this time, world politics would rearrange her life in years to come. But for now, digging potatoes was the chore.

The vegetable garden, which was a few yards from the back of the house, provided the family of seven with food for the year, especially for the harsh winter months. Jozefa was a productive wife for Pawel. Along with a fruitful garden which she harvested successfully, she gave birth to two fine sons and three lovely daughters. Unfortunately, the birth of her last child, Stanislawa, caused serious medical problems for Jozefa. Adults referred to these medical issues in disguised language since mention of a woman's medical health were not a topic for discussion in the 1920's in Poland, or in many other parts of the world. Since she had to be hospitalized in Wilno for three months, at tremendous cost to Pawel, including the forced sale of a fine cow, Jozefa's health was, from then on, not at its optimum. For the duration of her hospitalization, Maria, by then almost thirteen, became the caregiver for the infant Stanislawa, her father, two brothers, Aleksander and Stanislaw, and younger sister, Bronislawa. Maria never resented caring for her father or siblings, but felt an ache in her heart that she had to forego her schooling for a while.

Pawel worked hard on his seventy-five acre farm. He wasn't a rich man, but he provided all the necessities his family needed. His friends and neighbors saw him as a serious, God-fearing man who took his role as a father, neighbor, and friend earnestly. His wife and children viewed him quite differently depending on his mood on any given day. Men in this part of Poland were expected to rule their homes with severity and he was no different. He loved his wife, but thought nothing of using his hands to make sure she was subservient to him. He was overly strict with his sons, Aleksander and Stanislaw, but only threatened to give his girls a thrashing; though he never did. He only needed to give them a stern look and glance at the black horsewhip which hung on a peg on the wall and that was enough. Fortunately, Pawel had a good side to his personality and would joke around with his family when disposed to frolicking. When he went into Wilno to sell his produce, wheat, or alfalfa, he always returned with some cakes or trinkets for his children and wife. Once Maria begged him to bring her a real doll, not one made of rags and stuffed with hay like her mother had made for her. She waited all day for a special doll dressed in a fine silk dress with tiny leather shoes. Pawel returned that evening, but not with a pretty porcelain doll, but with a small statue of the Blessed Virgin. Of course, Maria could not express her disappointment to her deeply religious father, so she pretended to be thrilled with the gift, but her heart pined for a real doll.

In keeping with the architectural structure of farm homes built in the early 1900's in this part of Poland, Pawel and his family resided in a large house close to fifty feet in length and thirty feet in width. Built on a stone foundation, the walls were constructed of wood planks cut from the local forest. The floor was made of oak and Pawel was proud that it shone like glass as Jozefa kept it spotless. The front area of the home housed a pantry for the storage of flour, sugar, salt, and the other food necessary for daily meals. Since refrigeration had not been invented, foods that needed cold storage were kept alongside the home in underground storage cellars dug into the cold earth. Once inside, the front living area included a sitting area, and a dining room on one side and the kitchen on the other.

A large, floor to ceiling brick oven separated the living spaces and was the only source of heat in winter. The oven was very large because several loaves of bread had to fit inside for baking. The long oak   kitchen table was used not only for family mealtimes, but also to prepare food, knead dough, and prepare fruits, vegetables and meats for storage. Dishes, pots, and utensils were washed in a large wooden tub with water carried from the well and heated on the stove. The heated water was also used to fill a galvanized steel tub needed for bathing. Primitive as the bathing protocol was, everyone in the family washed thoroughly on a weekly basis. This ritual occurred on Saturdays in preparation for Sunday Mass.

At the back of the house, to the rear of the dining room and sitting area, Pawel and his wife shared a bed and slept separated from their children by a heavy curtain which hung behind a large wardrobe closet. In the children's area, there were two beds and a cradle. The boys slept in one bed and the girls shared the other. The baby slept in the cradle and eventually was given a small bed. All the mattresses were made of straw but complaints were never heard since no one had ever actually seen a store bought mattress. For some reason, none of the farmers in the village thought of creating walls internally to distinguish separate rooms; instead, home life took place in one large open space.

Pawel was considered well-to-do by his neighbors since he had a large home. He had hired a carpenter to make the furniture for the house including beds, clothing closets, chairs and tables. Tablecloths, towels, and bed linens were stored in a linen cabinet also made by the young craftsman. Jozefa taught her daughter, Maria, to weave linen thread from the flax which grew in their fields. This task was arduous, but one at which she was quite adept. Little did the young daughter know that a piece of the cloth she wove at such a young age would one day be passed on to her family. The retained carpenter also made a large china cabinet which was used to store dishes and glassware. This cabinet also housed other items including an ornate silver samovar, a large urn with a spigot at the base used to boil water for tea. Being very proud of this samovar, Pawel used it with great ceremony whenever guests were present. Maria never knew where this prized possession came from, but her father owned the only one in their village and probably in any other village in the area.

One day, when her mother had almost completed weaving a large piece of cloth that she hoped to have the tailor make into shirts for her husband and sons and dresses for her daughters, Pawel came in from the field with an angry expression on his face. Jozefa looked at her daughter and the look was enough for Maria to know something bad was about to happen.

"Jozefa, why isn't food on the table?" he asked sharply.

"Pawel, this isn't the usual time you come in from the fields, so I haven't started cooking. I've been busy weaving the last few hours." Pawel glared at his wife, walked over to the loom, pulled his knife from its leather sheath and sliced though all the threads in one stroke. Jozefa burst into tears. Maria whimpered from behind her mother's long, gray skirt as Pawel shouted, "Make me a meal, now!"

Jozefa moved as quickly as she could about the kitchen making her angry husband something to eat. She was petrified to question his actions or consider talking back since that would end in a beating. All she kept thinking about were the hours she put into preparing the threads for the loom and then designing her pattern, only to have it destroyed without reason. Of course, that night Pawel prayed before Maria's Blessed Virgin statue asking for the Lord's forgiveness over his quick temper, while his children and wife knelt on either side of him in forced prayer asking the Virgin to keep them away from Pawel when his dark mood struck.

Maria remembered an incident that her brother Stanislaw told her about in referring to their father's angry outbursts. Pawel's disciplinary beatings of his sons continued for many years until Stanislaw was about nineteen and quite strong. As he was working in the fields one day, Stanislaw saw his brother heading in the direction of the forest. He saw that Aleksander had a rope in his hand and wondered what his younger sibling was planning.

" Where are you going Aleks?" shouted Stanislaw as he caught up to his younger brother.

"I've had enough of father's black moods and with being whipped for no logical reason, so I'm going to hang myself."

"Hang yourself!" Stanislaw yelled incredulously.

"Aleks, you can't do this. Think what this will do to mother. She'll cry herself to death and father will still hit her and me at his whim. Listen to me, I beg you. Besides, our priest will not bury you, a suicide, in consecrated ground and God will not forgive you. Come home with me and somehow I'll protect you and mother," pleaded Stanislaw.

Aleksander listened to his older brother and returned home with him. Stanislaw kept his word. He approached his father, grabbed him by the shirt collar and swore he'd kill him if he ever touched any of them again. Somehow this worked and the beatings ended for Jozefa and her sons. Maria empathized with her brothers after she learned about this event, but as a teenager and a female, she was powerless to intervene.

Despite Pawel's days of anger, often caused by severe headaches, or at times very painful stomach aches, Pawel often helped his neighbors or anyone in need. Maria recalled one such incident which occurred during the mid 1930's. It was a difficult economic time in the world with the Great Depression in full swing in America. Europe was suffering as well and Poland was included in the economic devastation. Students were graduating from Polish universities but work was scarce. One day a young man stopped by the farm to ask for employment.

"Sir, I recently graduated from the University of Wilno

and I am seeking work since there is no employment in the city," stated the tall, gaunt, newly-hatched graduate to Pawel.

"Show me your hands son," remarked the farmer. "I see they are soft and clean and not capable of accomplishing the labor required on a farm," Pawel observed.

"This is true sir since I was a philosophy major, but maybe there is something I could learn here."

Pawel scratched his head and replied, "Philosophy will not get you work here or on any farm in the vicinity, but you seem like a clever young man so let me offer you an easy way to make a few zloty (Polish monetary units) until the economic climate improves and you can find work in your field."

The graduate listened attentively as Pawel presented a plan. "I will tell you about as many famers and their families in this region as I can and you will become an itinerant fortune teller. I know it sounds foolish but the women here will be glad to pay you a bit to tell their past and future. So I will teach you how to get a few home cooked meals and some cash in return for their curiosity. For example, the widowed-woman in the last house in our village wants to marry off her not so beautiful daughter. Provide her with hope, by telling her that a suitor will eventually arrive for her daughter. I happen to know that a young man from the neighboring town is interested, not so much in the girl, but in the land and will soon approach the lady to discuss marriage with the daughter. The widow will be thrilled and you will have attained some money and a meal," stated the grinning Pawel.

He then proceeded to fill the young man's brain with tidbits about everyone in the area. "Go now and make your temporary living. But remember, women love to gossip so be an attentive listener and remember all you are told in supposed secret. Use the information wisely and you might succeed at this." Both men laughed uproariously at this plan as the young man departed. Pawel knew that what he had done would have been considered a sin by his parish priest, but he saw it as aiding a fellow human being who had little hope of surviving in the present world.

Pawel was a progressive man for the time period and for the area in which he lived. His children were growing older and one day an idea came to him that would benefit them and other children of the village.

"Jozefa, we need a school here for our children," he declared.

"What are you talking about Pawel?"

"A school! I've thought about it and I want my children to read. My father taught me to read but I'm not really educated. I can read the Bible and my prayer book but this is the 1920's and the world is moving ahead so quickly. I'm going to get the village men together on Sunday and we'll discuss my idea."

So that Sunday, after church, the men gathered at Pawel's house.

"Pawel, how are we going to find a teacher?" inquired

Tomek who lived down the road.

"We'll talk to the mayor and ask him to pay for a teacher and I can go to Wilno to hire one," responded Pawel.

Mietek asked, "Where will she teach? We have no school and most of us can't afford to build a school right now."

Pawel was not going to give up so easily.

"Fine! I have a large house. I will section off the back one third and we can put tables, chairs, a blackboard, and a teacher's desk in that area. I will house the school and we can all work on the furnishings, but we must educate our sons and daughters. The school will be in my home until we can get the government to build this town a school," stated Pawel, authoritatively.

"Pawel, this is too much sacrifice on your part, but if you can do it, we will support you," Janek stated and shook Pawel's hand.

"But where will the teacher live, Pawel?" asked Marek, "We have no space in my home or, I'm sure, anyone else's either."

"You're right Marek," replied Pawel. "She will live in a small room I have for the storage of my tools in my barn. I will have Jozefa clean it up and the teacher can stay there for now. When the school is finished, we will make sure that she has a room to herself there."

And that was how Maria began her education! The young teacher, Miss Anna, was brought to Maria's home by Pawel to teach the local children. She lived with the family for almost a full year, until the one room schoolhouse was completed. Maria and her brothers and sisters were taken by her kindness and willingness to teach. She had a warmth about her that was special, especially toward Maria. After dinner, she sat with the children and read them poetry and stories which the youngsters grasped eagerly with their curious minds. Maria was bright and wanted to learn as much as possible. After Miss Anna left to get married, other teachers arrived and stayed for a year or two, but no one was as special to Maria as her first teacher.

During one year when Miss Janka was hired to teach classes, she inadvertently left a science book on her desk. Curiosity got the best of Maria and she started leafing through the book when the teacher left the room to bring in wood for the stove. At this ill-fated time, Pawel came into the room unbeknownst to Maria and saw her engrossed in looking at pictures of human anatomy – male and female. Even though Maria was almost a teenager, her father was shocked that books contained such drawings and that his child was looking at them. He grabbed the book out of his daughter's hands and flung it across the room. He struck his wide-eyed, petrified daughter and sent her home wailing as he shouted, "This is not for you to know about yet!"

Pawel called a meeting of the townsmen. After his report, Miss Janka was sent away without being permitted to explain why the children should learn facts about their bodily functions and structures. Pawel believed in educating the children to read, write, and do mathematics, but anatomy was not to be part of their learning experience.

When Maria was almost thirteen, her mother, Jozefa delivered her last child, a daughter named Stanislawa. A few weeks after her sister's birth, Pawel came to his daughter and informed her about Jozefa's serious illness. The village doctor, who was not really a medical doctor, but an army medic who returned from the First World War, could not help Jozefa. She needed to go to the hospital in Wilno, 30 kilometers away for treatment. But the farm needed a woman to care for the animals and the family.

"Maria, I am forced to take you out of school because someone has to help me with the chores at home. Your mother, along with the new baby, will be in the hospital a long time and I have to rely on you," her father stated seriously.

Maria could not sleep that whole night not only worrying about her mother, but also because she realized what work would be expected of her in terms of boiling potatoes for the pigs, feeding the cows, horses, and fowl, and caring for her siblings and father. But her sadness also included the realization that her education would not continue. She completed sixth grade and despite the hope that she would someday return to school and at least finish eighth grade, she had a premonition that this would never happen.

Maria proved to be a good replacement for her mother. After all, Jozefa taught her well and, despite her youth, she did what a farmer's wife had to do at that time. The only thing she couldn't do was put the freshly made loaves of bread she made into the oven. The loaves were large, weighing about ten pounds each. She had to knead about six every other day for her father, hungry siblings, and the farm hands. Therefore, her father or brothers had to help her place the bread inside the oven. As to preparing fodder for the pigs, chickens, and geese, Maria did the cooking in large pots and her father carried everything to the animals where he poured the mixture into large wooden troughs.

Jozefa remained in the hospital for almost three months. Money became tight since the cost was so high forcing Pawel to sell his best milking cow to pay for the medications. Maria never knew why her mother was so seriously ill. "It's a woman's issue," was all Pawel would say.

The day Jozefa returned home was a joyful one for everyone, especially Maria. But Jozefa was very weak and her daughter continued to care for the family for many months. Maria assumed that when her mother recuperated she would continue with her education. Unfortunately, her parents had other plans for their beautiful, blue-eyed daughter.

Chapter Two

"Maria, in a few weeks you will be fifteen. It is time for you to think about marriage," Pawel smiled as he said these words to his lovely young daughter. "After all, your mother married me at the age of sixteen and you are almost ready for marriage and motherhood. Your mother and I discussed this and we have decided to have parties here so you can meet eligible young men," stated Pawel as he twisted his mustache. Not that guests and parties were something foreign to Maria, since Pawel and his wife were well respected in the community and liked to entertain every once in a while. But now, Maria realized, these parties would have a purpose. Pawel would notify his relatives and friends that his oldest and favorite daughter would be accepting suitors. Maria possessed a warm, friendly personality. She was a pretty, slender, young lady with long dark-blonde hair which she wore braided down her back. She was skilled in all areas of farm labor, cooking, and sewing. Her father was sure that a suitor would come along soon of whom he would approve.

"Father, I am grateful that you are considering marriage for me, but I'm not sure I'm ready yet," responded Maria.

"Of course you are! You have proven yourself daughter. You can cook, sew, weave, and care for farm animals. Besides work on the farm, your teachers tell us that you have a sharp mind for learning. It will take time to find the proper husband for you, but I'm sure that within a year or a year and a half you will be a bride! And a lovely one at that!"

"Yes, father. I'm sure you will find the right person for me," was all Maria could say. After all, she did not have much choice in the matter. As she knew from a very young age, once her father decided something there would be no way to change his mind. Actually, in this time period, all daughters in the area married when their fathers decided and wed men their parents selected. She could never disobey either of her parents, least of all her father. And so the search for a proper husband began. Pawel and Jozefa held get-togethers and dances at the house after harvest season, during special holidays and in the summer. Furniture was removed from the house and chairs and benches were set up along the perimeter of the living area. Food and drink were bountiful and local town musicians were hired to play the popular Polish music of the country villages. Maria and her siblings enjoyed these events, but she was always nervous as to which eligible young man would arrive to seek her hand.

As was the custom of the area, a bachelor who was

interested in a young lady would arrive at the house, usually on a Sunday, to speak with the father. The suitor would bring a bottle of vodka and would then begin to discuss his desire to wed the daughter. He would indicate what he owned and could provide the young lady. If the father agreed to the arrangement, and this involved the size of the dowry in terms of money and farm animals to be given with the girl, the men shook hands over a glass of vodka and the agreement was made. The daughter had very little, if anything to say, and accepted her fate.

Pawel met with many young men and even some widowers before agreeing to a wedding between Maria and a young man from a neighboring village, known as Boleslaw or Bolek, which was his nickname. Bolek was about twenty-four, an only son who cared for his widowed mother and was in good standing in his village. His farm was about the size of Pawel's, so that made him quite eligible.

Maria and her sister, Bronislawa, also known as Bronia, spoke often about whom they wanted to marry even though the choice would not be theirs. But their sisterly conversations were never in depth since their young ages only warranted superficiality on the subject of marriage or young suitors in general. But Bronia was still curious when she learned that her sister was soon to be a bride.

"What do you think Maria?" asked her fourteen year old sister Bronia. "Do you want to marry him?"

"I suppose so. What choice do I really have? He is not

as handsome as I hoped, but not really ugly either. I will have to get used to him," replied the compliant young lady.

"Do you think you'll ever love him?" pressed Bronia out of curiosity.

"I don't know what love is actually, but I hope I will at least like him and make him a good wife," was Maria's blushing response.

Just after her sixteenth birthday in mid-March, the wedding banns were posted in the parish church indicating that in three weeks Maria and Bolek were to be married. During this time period anyone who objected to the marriage could approach the parish priest and state the impediment to the wedding. If it were serious, such as a previous marriage, the wedding could be called off.

That March, the winter snows were heavy and quite deep in Zoltuny. Normally, this would not be important since winters were always fierce in this area. But one week prior to Maria's wedding, she left Sunday Mass with Bolek and waited outside the church as he got the horse and sleigh ready to take her the three kilometers to her home. As she stepped into the snow-covered street, Bolek drove up with another passenger in his two seat sleigh, Lydia, a local girl.

"Maria, wait here while I drive Lydia home and then I will return to get you," stated her betrothed matter-of-factly.

Lydia lived at least two kilometers past Maria's house and it was already close to one-thirty. Bolek wouldn't be back for at least an hour, so Maria walked home behind

Bolek's sleigh. The young suitor returned to pick up Maria after his work of mercy for Lydia was completed.

"Maria get in the sleigh and I'll take you home," he announced happily.

"No, Bolek. If you start offering sleigh rides to young ladies before our wedding, what will you be capable of later? The wedding is off," she stated empathically and continued walking toward her home.

Bolek was stunned by her response and sat back in the seat red-faced.

"I'm home mother," she said as she entered the house. She was exhausted from walking through the deep snow in her heavy fur coat and leather boots.

"But where is Bolek? And why are you so tired looking?" questioned Jozefa.

By then her father had entered the kitchen and began listening as she told of her experience. After she relayed the facts, she stated sternly to her parents, "Cancel the wedding. If he's going to give another girl a lift instead of me, I fear he will not be loyal to me in the future."

Pawel gave his daughter a hug and said, "You are young, but you are wise. You have made the right decision."

Maria and Bolek never married even though he came to the house time and again to beg for forgiveness. But once Maria, like her father, made a decision, she stuck to it even if the consequences might not be the best.

Since the wedding never occurred, gossip spread that Maria was again available and a second group of suitors began to arrive. This time, Pawel found no appropriate man for his young daughter.

As fate would have it, Maria was asked to be the godmother to a family her parents knew from the neighboring village of Gierdziejewce. As was customary, one did not refuse such an honor since it would bring bad luck to the child. Besides this, Maria found out from her cousin, also named Maria, that the man who was to be the godfather of this child was a twenty-three year old handsome man from that same village. His name was Jozef and he was the eldest son in a family of twelve children and supposedly the hardest working of the lot. Maria looked forward to the event and also to meeting this young man. Of course, she could not make the decision to marry anyone. If Jozef were interested, and if her father found him favorable, a marriage could be a possibility. The only issue her father might have would be marrying his favorite daughter into such a large family since her life would not be easy. She would become an extra pair of hands to her mother-in-law and an extra worker in the fields. Before anything could happen, she had to first meet Jozef and see if they even liked each other.

Chapter Three

One look at Jozef, followed by a brief introduction prior to the Christening, was enough for Maria to believe she was in love. Of course, she spoke to him during the festivities and while they danced she got to know about him and his family, and he about hers. This chance encounter was enough to convince her that Jozef could be her husband.

"Mother, I want to marry Jozef!"

"Daughter, are you serious? You just met him a few hours ago at church and I saw you speaking to him at the celebration after the Christening. How could you be so sure in such a brief time?" questioned Jozefa.

"Mother, I just know that I want to spend my life with him. And, my cousins Zofia and Maria have heard that he is well-liked and respected in his village. He's been asked to be a godfather at least three times and you know that's a positive sign about the quality of a man."

"Well, your father needs to speak to him first and the final decision will be his," Jozefa stated straightforwardly.

Maria excluded some details about her feelings for Jozef such as his handsome face, clear blue eyes and blond hair. Of course, his physical labor on the family farm also created a well-structured physique which Maria also neglected to mention, but which she shared with her cousins, her sister Bronia, and her friends.

Jozef also found that there was something special about this blue-eyed, strawberry-blond young lady. He liked her smile and her sense of presence. She liked to talk, but her conversations were sensible. She also enjoyed dancing and singing which were two things he was fond of since he taught himself to play the harmonica – not very well, but well enough to accompany a singer or two.

Jozef asked Pawel's permission to visit the following Sunday to speak about his desire to marry Maria. Pawel agreed to the meeting and Jozef arrived in his best jacket and riding slacks, his glistening deep-brown leather boots and riding his favorite chestnut stallion.

"You're right my child. You have good taste in looks at least. Let's hope your father and Jozef get along and things work out. I know your father has great concerns about the number of siblings Jozef has and even though his father has a similar sized farm as ours, it will be divided among his three sons and of course some will be sold off to pay the dowries for Jozef's sisters. But we will see what your father says," stated her mother unemotionally.

Maria's facial expressions indicated that her mind was made up, no matter what Pawel decided. "I will marry him mother; father will not prevent this marriage," she stated firmly.

Jozefa looked at her eldest daughter and realized that Maria's mind was made up. "So be it child – as you say and as the Lord wills."

Despite the fact that her father had the last word as to whom Maria would marry, she convinced Pawel that Jozef was the husband for her. Since Pawel didn't want to disappoint his child, he relented and agreed to the marriage.

Between planting season and the August harvest, there was no time to make wedding preparations. But on Thursday, September 1st of 1930, Maria and Jozef were married at St. Michael's Church in Taboryszki. As was typical of village customs, the wedding celebration lasted from Thursday until Sunday night. Family and friends arrived from all directions by wagon and all had to be accommodated. Tables were set outside and inside the house with food prepared for days in advance by Jozefa, her daughters and of course, various aunts and cousins. A variety of farm animals had to be slaughtered, vegetables prepared, breads and cakes baked and vodka had to flow. The center of the house was emptied to prepare a dance floor and musicians played each evening entertaining the many guests. The weather was perfect, therefore, everyone slept in their wagons, on the blanket-covered grass, or in the upper level of the barn on heaping mounds of yellow straw which was spread on the floorboards. The local seamstress made Maria a simple white linen dress with lace trim along the collar and the cuffs. The young bride wore a wreath of fresh flowers over her floor length white veil. Jozef wore a new suit which he purchased in Wilno and he looked striking next to Maria's radiant glow. The bridesmaids, all in new dresses in the style of 1930, included Bronia, Maria's sister, and her cousins, Emilia and Maria. Jozef's brother, Jan, was the best man.

After the festivities at Pawel and Jozefa's home, the couple, along with Jozef's family hitched the horses to the wagons and drove the approximately five kilometers to their new place of residence in Jozef's father's house. There, they were provided with a bed and a chest of drawers at the rear of the house surrounded by a linen curtain which afforded them a moderate amount of privacy. Maria was not thrilled about this arrangement, but this was how life was for all families in all the villages around them. This was the only life she was familiar with and she accepted her fate.

Chapter Four

Jozef's parents, Pawel and Stefania, were quite different from Maria's parents. Both were God-fearing people who attended church weekly, but neither one was as fanatical about their faith as her father. The family was large since Stefania gave birth to thirteen children. However, only Jozef, Marian, Jan and six sisters Stanislawa, Janina, Wanda, Leokadia, Michalina and Jadwiga survived past infancy. The home was not as neat and orderly as Maria's since the mother was busy with the children and farm chores. Her husband worked on the farm until his sons were old enough to do the labor. Jozef actually began working beside his father at the age of seven. As Jozef told it, as he plowed the fields he was barely able to see over the horse's rump. By the time he married, he was responsible for running the whole farm while his father spent many hours fishing by the local river.

In actuality, Maria was simply another mouth to feed and as a daughter-in-law had little to say about anything. She was required to work the fields and help with cooking and cleaning. But, when it came to getting a glass of milk or a piece of bread with butter for herself, she had to ask permission since the cold storage cabinet was under lock and key. She learned not to ask since the in-laws and sisters-in-law would call her an ingrate, as if living with them were an honor.

Jozef told her that he would soon ask his father for his share of the land so he could start building his own house. He kept his word to his bride and after a year of pleading, his father agreed to give him the land. Jozef built a small cottage on the few acres and called it, "Nowo Alechnowo." A short time later, his father went back on his word and refused to sign over the property. He said he would do it sometime in the future. The young couple had no idea when that would happen. In reality, his father needed Jozef to run the farm. When his friends heard that Pawel allowed Jozef to move to the cottage some distance away from the main house, they questioned his rationale.

"What are you doing Pawel? This son is the most diligent of your sons and your eldest. If you allow him to go off on his own land, who will work your fields since your younger sons have no real interest in farming? Jan is going to agricultural school and is only interested in growing various fruit trees and working with his apiaries. Marian is still in his teenaged years and in school. You need a real work-hand and Jozef is that person. Bring him back here or your farm will fail," was the neighbors' chorus.

Pawel listened to his friends and after pleading with Jozef, his son and daughter-in-law returned to the main house. Their little one room cottage remained a dream of a future return.

Within the first year of their marriage Maria lost her first child, a son, due to a miscarriage. Over time she became pregnant with three daughters. Helena and Bronislawa grew into healthy, pretty little girls. Albina, the middle child, died at nine months from an undiagnosed illness.

After Albina's death, Maria was inconsolable. She visited the grave almost daily and sobbed over the loss of her little one. One day as she knelt at the grave, clutching the cross and weeping, a terrible wind erupted out of the clear blue sky. Maria was astonished as she wiped the tears from her eyes. As she looked up and gazed into the distance, she saw a figure dressed in a white gown approaching. The shocked young mother heard the personage say as it moved closer, "Don't weep. Your child is safe and at peace."

Maria asked the vision, "Who are you? Is my daughter in heaven?"

But the figure was gone from sight.

Maria wondered about this and told her husband and her parents about the phenomenon but they dismissed it all to her hysteria over the loss of Albina. She believed differently and kept this event in her heart always.

Her mother-in-law gave birth to her thirteenth child at the same time that Helena was born. All the while, everyone lived in the same two-room house and a second daughter-in-law was added when Jozef's brother married. Needless to say, life proved trying but she persevered in the belief that one day she and Jozef would again have their own home on part of her father-in-law's land.

The Invasion
of Poland
September 1, 1939

Chapter Five

In the spring and summer of 1939, the talk in the village related to the political situation in Europe. Hitler's Germany was on everybody's lips. Poland, historically, was always at the mercy of her two enemies – Germany on the West and Russia to the East. The townspeople feared that once again their country would be invaded by one or both countries depending on what the government leaders of those nations and in all of Europe decided. Poland was not a powerful nation. While Germany was building tanks, the Polish army was training its cavalry.

Jozef had been drafted into service prior to his marriage and served his country for two years. But if war broke out, he would be recalled into service despite the fact that he was thirty-two and the father of two. So when the men gathered in the village after church services, the conversation inevitably turned to the foreboding political climate in Europe. Jozef, and the other men, hoped that Hitler could be placated by world leaders without people dying. Yet, in their hearts they felt otherwise. As the summer months came to an end, Jozef received a military notice that if war broke out, he was to report to Army headquarters in Wilno. Jozef and Maria spoke daily about their future in the event of war, but they were powerless to control their lives. Each worried about the safety of the other and of their children and families, but all they could do at the moment was pray.

Unfortunately, in this situation, prayer did not change Hitler's mind. He ordered the invasion of his neighboring country and on September 1ˢᵗ his Panzer divisions attacked Poland from the West as his political ally in Russia, Stalin, attacked Poland from the East. Jozef was recalled to the military and hurried to Wilno to defend his country, but to no avail.

At one point, when her husband was at the battlefield for a few weeks, Maria left her daughters with her parents and walked the thirty kilometers to Wilno to find her husband and make sure he was alive.

Before she started out in the pre-dawn hours carrying a sack filled with bread, dried meat, and cheese for Jozef in case he was hungry, her father pleaded.

"Maria don't do this. It is far too dangerous for a young woman to walk to Wilno alone. You are risking your life," cried her father, fearing for her safety.

But she would not be swayed.

"I must see my husband even if it might be for the last time. He might need me. He could already be wounded. If something should happen to me father, care for my girls. I know I can count on you and mother." With her long wool shawl wrapped around her slender shoulders, her food satchel in hand, Maria walked down the dirt road to find her husband.

She stopped along the road to eat a hard-boiled egg and a slice of bread. Just before nightfall, she found a flat patch of ground behind a large oak and spread her small blanket on the earth. She used her burlap sack filled with food as a pillow and she fell asleep quite readily. In the early morning hours, the sun rose over the horizon and woke the weary traveler. She found a stream not far from the place of her repose where she washed the sleep out of her eyes. It was here in the verdant spot that Maria again ate a bit of bread and some cheese. Her hunger abated, she gathered her goods and proceeded on her walk toward Wilno. Though wolves were plentiful in the woods, luckily, she survived the night unharmed. When she arrived in the morning, Maria went to the military barracks to inquire about Jozef. The commanding officer pointed her in the direction of the tent where her husband was housed. She found him talking to some of the men in his company.

"Maria what are you doing here?" Jozef asked incredulously.

"I walked here to bring you something to eat since everyone in the village says our soldiers have little to eat. I also wanted to make sure you were alive and not wounded."

Jozef hugged his wife and assured her that he was well physically, but that he and the men realized they could not fight the enemy much longer since they were so ill prepared. This knowledge caused some men to become depressed and fearful and a few had already gone back to their villages to defend their families.

"Are you leaving also Jozef?" Maria questioned.

"No, Maria. I will not leave unless I am absolutely convinced that we cannot defend ourselves and our officers command us to do so. At this time, I still have hope; therefore, I will stay and fight," affirmed the resolute soldier.

After a few hours of talking about the children and family members, Jozef told Maria to return to the farm. There was no place for her in the army camp and she needed to be with their family. The two parted tearfully with Jozef promising that he would do his utmost to return home. Of course, they knew this might not be the case, but they hoped and prayed that all would end well.

With the information she had received from Jozef, Maria returned to her home and relayed what she had learned to her in-laws and her own parents. Everyone feared the future, but tried to live their lives with the hope that the war would end quickly and that their lives would normalize.

Chapter 6

The villagers' lives took a sharp turn when the Germans invaded the area. As they came through the various hamlets, the German soldiers took whatever foodstuffs they wanted. They also searched each home and barn for Jews. If they found that anyone had harbored a Jewish person, the Polish family was shot and even entire villages were burned to the ground. At this point, no one knew that Hitler was rounding up Jewish people for his grand plan of exterminating their race along with other "undesirables." Everyone heard rumors but nothing specific had yet been known.

During the early months of the war, Maria's father secretly hid a Jewish man on his forest lands. He brought him food every few days for many weeks, but one day he found the poor man had committed suicide by hanging. Pawel cut him down from the tree limb and buried the man near the oak tree under some thick underbrush. While saying a few prayers, since he believed that the God of the Jews was the same as the one he worshipped, he requested that God grant the man eternal rest. The brief note left by the despondent man stated simply, "It is no use. You cannot hide me forever, so I am repaying your kindness. Protect yourself and your loved ones."

Many years later, Maria found out that her father was beaten severely by the Germans because they discovered that he and his sons helped Jews escape to Russia and Lithuania. After Pawel's severe beating, the German soldiers were about to shoot him when orders came to leave the area immediately and not waste a good bullet on Polish scum. Though before they left, they did take a moment to torch the interior of his home. Thankfully, her father survived.

Once the Germans left the area, the Russian troops arrived. They weren't as interested in killing Jews as they were in rounding them up along with Polish men and women and sending them into Russian slave labor camps. Throughout the areas these soldiers marched, the land became devoid of cattle, horses, foodstuffs and any objects that caught the eye of the commanding officers. Even Pawel's treasured samovar, stolen before his home was torched, made its way to some soldier's home. The only thing the villagers could do was hide what they could in their forests or bury them in the earth. The Russians had no interest in traipsing through dense Polish forests in search of hidden property.

Maria's brothers escaped deportation to Siberia by hiding in the forests. On the other hand, her husband's brother, Marian, went into hiding while Jan was captured by the Germans and sent to labor camps in Germany. Her father and father-in-law were too elderly to be of value to the Russians as slave laborers so they were spared, as were the women from both families. Unfortunately, Maria and her Jozef suffered a different fate.

Maria was already informed about her future from an event that had happened years prior. When she was about fourteen, a gypsy caravan passed through her village. The gypsy men repaired pots and pans, and stole whatever they could. The women went from house to house telling fortunes.

"Where is the lady of the house?" questioned the brightly clad gypsy. Maria surmised that the woman was probably around fifty years old since she was missing a couple of teeth and her hair was almost entirely gray.

"What is it you can tell us old woman," asked Jozefa.

"I've come to tell you your future, woman. And I will also tell the pretty girl hers since I have strong feelings about her." Maria was the only daughter home at the time since her sisters were playing in the garden, so she knew the old gypsy was referring to her.

"Fine," answered Jozefa, "What do you want in return?"

"I want three healthy chickens for reading your cards."

"Three! No, but two I can spare," replied Jozefa knowing that she couldn't suggest only one since the gypsy would steal another. But two would placate the fortune teller. So the gypsy began her session by laying out her well-worn cards. Her livelihood was evident in cards that passed through hundreds of villages and predicted the fate of many a farmer's wife.

Maria paid little attention to what the gypsy said to her mother, but when her turn came she hung onto every word.

"Your life will follow a different path than that of your mother my child," the gypsy stated.

"You will marry a fine young man, blond and blue-eyed and you will have many daughters. Your children will be with you for a while, but then a terrible time will come and you will be taken from here and sent far away from those you love. You will suffer a great deal and experience places you never dreamed of and meet many unusual people," stated the toothless, disheveled gypsy with a seriousness in her facial expression that took on an ominous air.

Maria took this all in but she was confused. "Mother, do gypsies always know the future?"

"Of course not! What she told you is simply impossible. Some of what she told you will of course happen – marriage, children, a fine husband. But the rest is ridiculous. She was only trying to get the two chickens, so I had to humor her. Just forget what the old hag said. This is how she makes her living – fabricating stories and stealing whatever she can. After all, if she doesn't bring something back to her camp, her husband will beat her. So at least we've prevented that for the fortuneteller."

Maria listened to her mother and put the gypsy's words

into the recesses of her mind. She did have hope for a fine blue-eyed husband and that comment she kept in her mind for the next few years. When she met Jozef with his blue eyes and blond hair, she believed the words the gypsy spoke or at least the portion about her future mate. The rest of the gypsy's message she forgot about until many years later.

Chapter Seven

One early morning, Maria spied a disheveled, tired looking man walking slowly toward the farm house. At first, she thought it might be a Russian or German soldier separated from his unit. The coat he wore was dusty and olive-green in color. It could have been the attire of any army. But as he drew closer, she recognized Jozef and ran toward him.

"My God, you're home!" she whimpered through teary eyes in a quivering voice.

"I left – we were losing terribly. You can't fight tanks with horses and rifles. Wilno fell before any of us could defend the city. Our officers told us to go home and try to defend our homes and families. I'm tired and hungry and still in disbelief. Maria, I don't know what will happen to us. We have to come up with a plan, but now I need to rest."

Maria helped her husband get settled, made him some potatoes and a bit of meat, and listened as he told his parents and siblings about his war experiences, brief as they were.

Despite the fact that Russian soldiers now occupied

the area, Jozef spent the fall and winter months of 1939 into early 1940 in typical farm labor – mending fences and broken barn boards, caring for the livestock, storing food for the bitter winter months to come and helping his wife with their young daughters. No one knew what the future would bring, but it was certain that nothing good would happen.

Skirmishes were conducted by local partisans against the Russian soldiers in the vicinity and all the townspeople were fearful since the killing of a soldier meant that local farmers could be arrested either alone or with their families. Townspeople could also be killed depending on the whims of the conquering army. Farms and homes were in danger of being burned, while cattle and horses could be taken. Already, small farm animals slowly disappeared only to appear on a Russian captain or general's table.

Jozef and his wife secretly hid as much grain and potatoes as they could in deeply dug pits throughout the farm. They had one milk cow left only because Jozef's mother pleaded with the soldier who was about to take the cow by pointing out that her still young children and grandchildren would starve. No one knew why the soldier took pity, but he left the cow and two horses. Maybe he hoped someone would do the same for his family. Nevertheless, the family hoped and prayed to survive at least until spring when the situation might change.

As the days grew closer to the Easter season of 1940, Jozef received information from a trusted friend in his village that his name and that of his family appeared on a list for resettlement to Russia. He knew enough that resettlement meant a possible separation from his wife and children and years of hard labor in Soviet prison camps for all of them. He was expecting this since he was the eldest son and would have one day inherited a good portion of his father's land. The Soviet government did not tolerate land ownership by individuals. So Jozef knew the inevitable was coming. Therefore, he had to plan quickly since arrest was imminent.

That night, he and Maria decided to gather their most necessary belongings and load them into their wagon. Along with Helena, who was now seven, and Bronislawa, a tiny three year old, they fled toward the city of Wilno and hoped to disappear in the bedlam of the metropolis. But first, they had to cross the newly drawn border between Russia and Poland. Unfortunately, this border ran right through the middle of their farm.

The young family fled Jozef's parents' home in the dark of night on Holy Thursday, the feast day before Easter Sunday. They arrived at Maria's parents' farm with the intention of continuing on their journey the next day after they and their horse rested. Jozef walked the horse to the barn, a beautiful black stallion about eighteen hands high. They knew each other well since Jozef had this horse from the day he was foaled seven years ago on their farm. As Jozef started to feed him, he noticed the horse staring at him and tears started falling from the animal's lovely black eyes. Jozef too started to cry as he and the animal sensed their fates. Both perceived that a terrible parting awaited them.

Chapter Eight

In the middle of the night, on Good Friday, March 22nd, 1940, the occupants at Maria's family home heard a loud banging on the farmhouse door. Maria's father moved quickly to open the latch. Four burly Lithuanian soldiers with rifles drawn entered and demanded that Jozef and his family dress, pack a few belongings in the next hour, and follow them. They were being arrested. Pawel and Jozefa begged and pleaded to no avail. Their orders were final and eventually this family would be handed over to Russian soldiers. But for now, the Lithuanian soldiers were to take them to the local prison a few kilometers away. The family was loaded into a wagon and taken to the estate of Mr. Tartaly, a local wealthy farmer, whose house was used to hold those who were arrested. Jozefa gave her terrified daughter a sack of bread and dried meat for the family and promised to bring more in the next day or so. This night was terribly cold; one of the worst Polish winters, so Maria took warm clothing and wool shawls for everyone. She hoped and prayed that these items would not be confiscated.

When they arrived at Mr. Tartaly's home, they discovered that there were many other families already there and awaiting their fate. The families were all forced into a dark and musty basement. Since it was a dusty cellar without windows, sunlight was not visible. Only a small kerosene lamp provided a bit of light. Straw was strewn on the dark-grey cement floor, though some was gathered and put into small mounds which made it more comfortable for the women and children to sit on or sleep. That was the extent of the comfort. A bucket was visible in the corner and was used as the toilet for all present. Maria looked at the bucket, but was too ashamed to use it. However, in due time her modesty lost out to the necessity of basic needs.

Water was provided once a day by the soldiers along with a little bread and a gruel-like soup. Maria tried to hoard the food she brought because she didn't know what the next few days or weeks would bring. She and her cellmates shared their fears about the future. Some of the prisoners heard stories from other people and spoke about what they thought they knew. But in reality, no one knew their fate and silently begged God for mercy.

Mercy came for Maria and Jozef's daughters. Maria's father-in-law arrived at the jail a few days after the arrest of his family and somehow was able to talk the commandant of the prison into freeing the girls. The truth was never discovered, but bribery was at the top on the list of reasons for the gesture of generosity. Generally, when a family was arrested, no one was sent back to their respective family.

Maria tried not to cry in front of her children but this was an impossible task. The girls were too young to understand what was happening, but despite loving their grandfather, they too were heartbroken by the separation.

"Mama, we don't want to leave you and father," cried Helena. Little Bronia sobbed and held fast to her mother's neck.

"I love you so much, but it is safer for you to go to your grandparents. When this war is over, we will have you back with us," she promised through tearful eyes.

"I will pray every day that God and the Blessed Mother protect you from harm. You must pray for us also," the sobbing mother requested.

As the girls cried, saying, "We will, we promise," the soldier gruffly yanked them out of Maria's arms and turned them over to their grandfather.

As the carriage pulled away, the girls stared through tearful eyes and waved their little arms in the direction of their parents. Maria was clinging to Jozef and collapsing in his arms as she cried uncontrollably. Her husband's kind, reassuring words and those of the other women in the cell fell on deaf ears. Everyone felt her pain and despite the gestures of comfort, everyone started weeping, especially the women.

Once their daughters were taken back home, life for Maria and Jozef became horrific. They both realized that the chances of seeing Bronislawa and Helena were negligible. Of course, they lived with hope and constant prayer, but the reality of the situation presented itself quite differently.

A week went by before this group of prisoners was moved out of the cell and taken by farm wagons to waiting cattle cars at the rail lines and eventually delivered into Russian military hands at Stara Wilejka, a town unknown to them. Enough prisoners had to be rounded up so that all the boxcars on the train were filled to the allotted capacity.

As Maria and her husband were herded into the car, they glanced ahead and to the rear to see how many cars there actually were.

"Can you count the number of cars Jozef?" she inquired.

"There is no beginning and no end I can see; but, at least thirty or more," he responded.

As they were pushed into the railroad car, they quickly scrambled for their own space on one of the wooden bunks which the soldiers called "pryczki." Jozef tried to find a window, but there was none. One of the slats at the top of the car was broken off so some light came in. Otherwise, there was little air or light for the dozens of people in the car. Each car was stuffed with fifty to seventy people of various ages – from children to old persons. There was a pot-bellied stove in the center of the car to provide heat and the men took turns keeping the fire aflame. At one end of the car there was a circular hole that was cut into the floor that was used as a latrine. If you had to use this facility, you asked someone to stand in front of you for modesty. Meantime, your family member remained in your tiny bunk area protecting your few belongings from theft. After all, you couldn't trust anyone since everyone was a stranger and their backgrounds were as varied as the sands in a desert. There were farmers, like Maria and Jozef, nurses, teachers, office workers, priests, nuns, housemaids, and even remaining members of the aristocracy not killed during the Russian Revolution. The Soviets arrested everyone without discrimination. Various religions were also represented, among them: Catholics, Jews, Orthodox Russians, Protestants, Baptists, and Jehovah Witnesses. The Soviet's purpose was to destroy the Poland everyone knew prior to 1939, and restructure the nation into a Communist satellite. At the same time, Russia was provided with slave laborers for the forests, mines, and factories so that all able-bodied Russian men could fight against the Allies.

At the Stara Wilejka train depot, Jozef was taken away for a week. Maria never found out what happened during this period. She surmised that he was being interrogated and beaten, since that was what happened to many prisoners, but he never divulged this information to his wife. They were imprisoned in this jail for three months, although not in the same cell. She saw Jozef a few times on her way to the latrines or the washrooms.

After their sojourn at this prison, the prisoners were moved again to another jail, but the name escaped Maria, where again the men and women were quartered separately.

Maria found herself in a dark cell with almost thirty women even though the cell had room for seven to ten people. At night, while some women took turns sleeping on the cold cement floor, others sat or stood around the perimeter of the cell. This draining ordeal lasted for three months and again they were moved to a jail in a place named Potock.

Life in each prison followed the same routine. Everyone was given a cup of water or boiled soup once a day along with a small piece of bread. The women were also marched to a latrine once a day and they were provided with a bucket of water daily for washing themselves. Unfortunately, everyone in the cell used the same bucket, consequently, the water became filthy very quickly. The women used pieces of torn clothing taken from the meager possessions they brought with them, and which the soldiers had not confiscated, with which to wash themselves.

Their time in Potock was not that long, just a couple of weeks. As the women were herded into cattle cars, Maria spied Jozef; nevertheless, she was forbidden to speak to him on orders from gruff, heavily armed Russian soldiers. Like the prisoners, the soldiers were cold and tired and expressed no sympathy for the people under their command. Maria noticed that Jozef, hunched over and bearded, looked worn out from his experiences just as she and the others around her.

During the grueling trip toward Moscow and further imprisonment, Maria cried daily for her family. When she wasn't sobbing, she prayed or tried to sleep. Food, while in

47

transit, was at a minimum and what was doled out provided little nourishment. The daily ration consisted of a cup of soup, which was hot water, a miniscule piece of fish, far too salty, and a slice of bread. A barrel, containing water for drinking, stood in the corner of the car but only caused vomiting since it was generally dirty. A hole cut in the floor at one end of the car was used as a toilet; however, there was absolutely no privacy. By this time in their journey, no one cared.

As the elderly began to grow more feeble from this forced diet, some lost their vision, some developed dysentery, while many others died. When the train stopped to refuel or to move aside for military transports, which had priority, bodies were thrown out along the tracks. If the train stopped at actual train stations, the local townspeople were commandeered to bury the dead in communal graves. Bodies of infants or children, who died en route, were discarded by their mothers like garbage when the trains slowed down. If the bodies weren't buried by the local peasants, wild animals and birds dragged them off. The sorrow and anguish endured by these mothers was beyond comprehension and many went into depression, refused to eat, and joined their babies in unmarked graves.

Maria knew in her heart that her daughters would be safe and cared for by her parents, unfortunately, she could not reconcile her grief. Jozef, in another cattle car, hoped that at least he and Maria would not be separated once they arrived at their next prison. But he had no way of knowing their future. He refused to listen to the horror stories that were rampant on the journey of torture, rape, and inevitable starvation facing both men and women prisoners.

Jozef lost track of time during the duration of the nightmare on the train. He sensed that at least two weeks had gone by before the motley group arrived in the train yard on the outskirts of Moscow.

As the doors to each car opened, soldiers yelled for all to disembark. Maria held onto another women's hand as they jumped off into the slushy snow. An angry older soldier pushed the men into one line and the women into another. It was one of the last times Maria saw Jozef's hand waving in the distance. The look in her eyes was of pure fear at possibly never seeing his cool, blue eyes again. Suddenly, hearing the soldiers barking orders within earshot brought her back to the reality of the moment. The two parallel lines of prisoners were forced to march from the rail station to another lice infested jail. It was freezing and all were starving, but they marched on. How long this forced exercise took, Maria couldn't remember since her mind was as frozen as her body.

Finally, they arrived at a prison in Moscow where the men were directed to one part of the courtyard and the women to the other. Even though she could not see Jozef, Maria could feel his presence.

The women were led to a large holding area in groups of about a hundred and forced to turn over all personal items. They were each given a coarse prison dress, a quilted jacket, and a blanket. They were permitted to keep their shoes and undergarments.

At this point, about twenty to thirty women were again marched to a cell which was similar to ones in the past and which should only house about ten people. They were ordered to make a place for themselves on the cold cement floor. Maria huddled against a damp wall and this spot became her place of semi-refuge for the next few weeks. Time had no real meaning here and actually no one cared or kept track of days or months. The only thing anyone kept track of was food. Rations of soup arrived daily in large buckets, that is, the so called soup. The prisoners called it "kipitok" because all it consisted of was boiled water, a few bits of oats, and, on a good day, a fish head or bones. Along with this delicacy, everyone received a slice of rye bread which was always hard and sometimes stale. This was the highlight of each day and the bread was savored like the finest cuisine.

Once a day, all the women were marched from the cells to the latrines. During one of these visits, Maria heard her husband whispering her name from the latrines on the other side of the wooden wall. All Jozef could say in the brief encounter was that he hadn't been tortured, and that he knew they would, one day, get out of this hell and be together. This kept Maria's spirits up, at least for a while.

If a woman had an emergency and needed to use the latrines, she had to beg the cell guard. On one occasion, Maria asked to leave the cell for this purpose. Instead of being taken to the latrine, the guard took her to the center of the courtyard and told her to squat under a tree as the other soldiers laughed at her and the German shepherds growled and barked. Maria was so afraid and humiliated that she couldn't relieve herself. She never asked to use the latrine again, instead waiting her turn with the other women in her cell.

As if the meager diet were not enough, the lack of sleep added to the terror of prison life. Since there were so many women in a cell generally meant for only a few, everyone was forced to sleep on one side of her body. Every couple of hours, on the command of the guard, the women were ordered to switch to the opposite position. No one slept on her back as this would crowd the other prisoners. During these sleepless nights, another added torment was the constant attack of lice. These creatures crawled through every crevice of a person's body and bit the prisoners unmercifully. There was absolutely no escape from the feasting bugs since hygiene was nonexistent.

The only positive aspect of this ordeal was that the women did not have to experience their menstral cycles since their lack of proper nutrition caused a cessation of this female issue. There were no proper products for these women, other than rags, should their cycles return.

The final fear came on a nightly basis as different women were forcibly removed for interrogation. Sometimes it was the same woman for a few days in a row. Eventually, everyone was interrogated. Some women were beaten, some verbally assaulted and a few raped. But rape was rare as far as Maria knew, unless the women were too frightened to say. Polish Catholic women were reticent about speaking of sexual abuse since sex was considered sacred and if a woman were violated she kept this a secret. The women feared that if their loved ones found out, they would be ostracized as possibly being complicit in the act. But everyone came back from being interrogated scarred in some way, either physically or psychologically.

One night, Maria heard the outer doors screeching open and the clicking sound of boots marching on the pavement heading in the direction of the cell area. Maria could feel the terror in the air as each of her fellow prisoners sat up waiting to see if the door to their particular prison cell would be flung open and an inmate selected. She could feel the hairs on the back of her neck stand on end. She knew more hairs on her head would turn gray this night and join the army of others that already covered her head.

Just then everyone heard the sound of the key turn in the rusted lock. The cell door swung open and the women froze as the soldier in charge called out, "Maria Pavlovna Pawlukiewiczovna." It was the Russian version of Maria's name that rang out. She could sense the relief in the other women as she rose to her feet for another night of numbing questioning and moved her cold trembling body toward the door. She couldn't even protest. Her tongue couldn't move in her mouth. Like one of the calves led to slaughter on her family's farm, she stepped between the two hulking soldiers and proceeded on one of the many all-night interrogations conducted in the lowest depths of this living hell.

Maria's frail body began to shake as the two somber soldiers began to march her down the dark, musty corridor. They came to a door which one of the soldiers opened and proceeded to descend the cold brick staircase to the lower levels of the prison. Even in her fear, she realized they were going down at least two floors to the bottom depths of the dungeon. Once there, they entered a dimly lit hallway that led to a corridor leading to the left and right. They turned to the left and Maria continued along as fearfully as a rabbit trapped by a hunter. Rows of iron clad wooden doors were visible on both sides of the hallway. It wasn't the doors or passageways that terrorized her, but the sounds that emanated from behind each portal. Both male and female voices pleaded for help, screamed from the pain of torture, and questioned why they were being beaten.

"I know nothing, please don't hurt me anymore," she heard coming from behind a door as she passed by.

"I'll tell you whatever you want," yelled another, as a rubber truncheon smacked against human flesh. She began to shiver and could feel the tears beginning to well up in her eyes. "Was this what they intended to do to me? God help me," she prayed silently.

The chamber into which Maria was led was similar to her cell. The only difference was that here she was totally alone. The guards who marched her down here were present and so was the interrogator, but they were not here to quench her need for human presence.

In her previous cell at least, she was among thirty or so women who were as terrified as she; however, there was a unique camaraderie that united them. They were acquaintances to the same horror, but were also fearful of each other since there was at least one spy in each cell. The question was "who?" Now, she had a new fear to face.

The dark grey walls of this cell drew Maria back to the realization as to why she was here. She stared at the sparsely furnished surroundings. Two chairs, an old wooden desk on which she saw a ledger-like book opened to the first few pages, and a large water pitcher and glass were the only items she noticed through her fear.

"What do they want from me, I'm no one special," she thought? " I've only had a sixth grade education and then at sixteen I became a wife and soon after a mother. She and Jozef were farmers – not intelligentsia or aristocrats by any means," she kept thinking to herself.

"Oh God," she whispered, "Here he comes."

The same soldier who had interrogated her a few days ago was her inquisitor again. He was crueler than the old, fat one whom she remembered from the last few days. This one was tall and slim, with angular facial features. He had small, dark eyes, like that of a blackbird, which darted here and there. His lips, almost white because they were closed so tightly, quivered slightly. There was no compassion in his face, yet he wore a wedding band. It was impossible to picture him caressing his wife or rocking his children to sleep. That was a side of him that she couldn't imagine as he began to probe into her frail mind.

On the war front, there are bullets ripping muscle and bones. Here, words flew from all directions and tore at the core of Maria's brain.

She was forced to sit in the rickety chair in front of the desk as the interrogator started to question her again.

"Speak. Tell us you're a spy. Confess because we already know the truth."

What truth was he after? What did she know? She could only tell him in which fields they planted wheat last year and how much was harvested. Did he think she spied on her neighbor? No need to. She knew, and had always known, how many cows, chickens, and pigs he had and that he fooled around with his maid every time his wife was pregnant, which was often. So what could she spy about? Maria didn't know. All she heard resoundingly were his words over and over again like the rat-tat-tat of a distant machine gun. The yelling, cursing, and smacking across her legs with his rubber truncheon did not change her story. She, her husband and children crossed the border from her father-in-law's farm to her father's home, only a few kilometers one from the other, and then they planned to travel to Wilno to get work. Both parents had too many mouths to feed and not enough food due to the war. She said this over and over in a mixture of Polish and the little Russian she learned thus far.

Suddenly, she was yanked off the chair painfully by her

hair after about an hour of torment, and gruffly marched back to her cell. Maria was now a drained, pale, shell of a woman, wife and mother. She wondered about death – why hadn't it come for her? She had had enough. Maria was twenty-six and turning gray after only a few months on trains, various prison cells and now in this horrendous place. The worst was the not knowing. Would they drag her down tomorrow, would they rape or torture her, or would she be shot? Where was her husband, her children, her family? Questions, but no answers. A living-hell!!

She thought about the scripture quote, "He descended into hell" and wondered, "is this it; am I doomed here for eternity?" She contemplated as to what her priest would say. Was this her punishment for her horrible sins? But what were they to warrant such an inferno - certainly not sins of the flesh. Who had thoughts of such things when one was constantly weary from working the fields, birthing children, and pleasing her husband and his family? So what sins was she paying for? Maybe none so horrible; maybe this was just her fate.

Maria's exhausted body was marched back to her cell where some of the women tried to comfort her. She had barely closed her eyes when morning came and one of her cellmates tried to force some soup and bread into her mouth.

"Stop trying to feed me. I want to die and end this horror," Maria said as she pushed away the hand of an emaciated woman sitting next to her. The lady was older than she by about ten years, but while suffering this ordeal resembled a skeleton with a mop of gray hair. The woman tried to shove a spoon, of what was supposed to be soup, into Maria's mouth. Maria knew that the gaunt women's name was Anna and she remembered bits and pieces of what she told Maria about herself - a spinster – once engaged – her fiancée killed in a freak farm accident – taught school in a small farming community – a pleasant person. Anna kept talking to her and insisting with every spoonful that Maria must survive. Her family would need her once she got out of this abyss. But how could Maria explain to Anna that she was tired? Deep down tired to the very bones of her being! She couldn't even think about living anymore, but Anna persisted.

"One spoon for Helena, one for Bronia, one for your mother, one for your father, one for your husband," Anna continued force feeding the depressed non-verbal Maria.

Maria's eyes darted to the four corners of the cell. The terrorized women were all jammed one next to the other, like so many fish in a tin. Behind her a message was scrawled into the cement wall, written by a priest. There was a name and a date – Father Michal A. – 1939. There was also a prayer – a long one begging for grace and blessing and written in Polish. She read it over and over, but couldn't seem to comprehend any of it. It didn't matter. She muttered a prayer she knew well every minute, but help still hadn't arrived.

Maria had an unusual dream one night which she

imparted on her cellmate Anna.

"I saw myself in a dark, deep pit in a murky, gloomy valley and I was alone. Gray, angry looking rocks were all around me. There was not a blade of grass or a flower or even the sound of a chirping bird. As I walked through this desolate underworld, I saw a large black cross standing on a hill ahead of me. It towered over me and I felt so slight in its shadow. Within seconds, it fell at my feet without striking me and I shrieked in fear. What do you think it means Anna?"

"It is a positive dream Maria. It shows that you are in a dark place, like this prison but the cross you saw is still before you. Since it fell down, I think one day you will get out of this hell and the cross you now bear will fall away from you. There is hope for you yet, so don't despair. You will see your family again."

Maria wasn't sure what to believe, but Anna's elucidation of her dream gave her hope. With this heartening dream, and Anna's words about the future, she started to eat on her own and build up her strength.

Maria believed that her only other hope was in God; therefore, she prayed fervently daily. She had no rosary but she made one for herself, and other women, by taking a thread from the bottom of her potato-sack dress and stringing beads, which she formed from pieces of bread and spit. She started her task with a formed cross, let that dry on the string and continued with the Our Fathers and Hail Marys. This process took days since she only received a small slice of bread daily, but she made do with less food so as to have a rosary. This had to be done in secret and hidden, otherwise she would be shot. Her home-made brown-bread rosaries lasted for years and were a reminder of her struggle. She hoped that one day her supplications to God would set her free and she could see her family. But often, her prayers were simply mumbled in rote and she wondered if almighty God accepted them. Only time would tell.

It was now November or December of 1940, Maria was not sure since the days and weeks blended into one time frame. One day, as the women sat huddled in their cramped, filthy cell, the situation changed for the prisoners.

"Come on you Polish whores," yelled the cell keeper one morning. "You're going to your trials."

The anxious women filed into a large room in the prison where an Army officer sat at a large, old wooden desk. There were soldiers standing around the perimeter of the room in case any women decided to bolt. Considering that they were all starving and lacking strength, this seemed ludicrous, but obviously, the soldiers' fearsome stance was meant as a show of Soviet power.

As their names were called, each woman advanced toward the desk and received her sentence. Maria's turn came and she too approached the officer who was now her judge and jury. She saw a document written in Russian on the desk and a pistol.

"Maria Pavlovna Pawliewiczovna, you have been

59

properly questioned and it has been determined that you attempted to cross the border of the Soviet Union into Poland for the purpose of spying against the motherland. By signing this document, you are agreeing to accept your sentence of five years of hard labor," stated the officer in Russian. Maria did not understand most of it, but one of the women who spoke Russian interpreted the statement to her. Like everyone else before her, she signed with her shaky, emaciated fingers and thanked the man for the brevity of the sentence.

The following morning the women were told to gather their blankets and few belongings and were marched to the railway station. Various groups of women were herded into one set of cattle cars while others were forced into cars on parallel tracks. Hundreds of railway cars lined the miles of tracks. No one provided the women with information concerning their destination.

Suddenly, out of the gray morning, Maria heard her name called by a familiar voice.

"Maria, it's me Jozef, to your right."

She saw her husband in a long line of men and began to cry. Jozef had lost many pounds during his sojourn in prison. He had dark circles under his eyes and a beard, but he still smiled at his wife and tried to cheer her up. She was too far a distance away to be able to speak to him and it was forbidden, nevertheless she knew now that he too had survived thus far.

Jozef held up his hand and showed her five fingers, so

she understood that his prison sentence was equal to hers. She gave him the same information by indicating the years of her sentence with her bony fingers held high. As the two lines of male and female prisioners passed each other, Jozef spoke a couple of words of hope to his tearful wife and then they were forced to continue marching. She had no idea where he was being sent and could not share with Jozef any information about her future destination. But at least they were both alive.

The Journey

Chapter Ten

The women were shoved into the dark, smelly, filthy cattle cars and soon discovered that the train was headed further into the Soviet Union.

"Maria sit here," yelled a voice from the corner of the railcar.

It was Anna, Maria's cellmate and caretaker. Maria's eyes slowly adjusted to the darkness in the train car as she pushed her way toward Anna. They embraced each other warmly and finally sat down in the corner on a dirty, straw covered wooden floor.

"Where will they take us Anna?"

"Probably to some God-forsaken wilderness where the devil said goodnight, Maria!" jeered Anna. Maria and the others in their vicinity continued to ponder Anna's words.

"Yes, to some horrible place where the devil laughs and God weeps," cried out another prisoner.

"I know Russia is a huge country. I remember seeing maps when I was in school," stated Anna.

"Yes, it stretches all the way to China," emphasized an

older woman, "I recall my father telling me this."

"I heard the guards speaking about a place named Orszy," commented another woman.

But this would not be.

"This train could take us to places and climates unfamiliar to us, nevertheless we must be strong, have faith, obey the rules, and maybe, God willing, we will survive and return to our homes. This odyssey of ours is not God's plan. It is the work of Hitler and Stalin. They are the devils whose evil plan has uprooted us from our country and sent us to who knows where," stated Anna emphatically before the train began to jerk forward.

"Be careful what you say Anna. There are collaborators on these trains who can report you. You will be shot without mercy," whispered the woman sitting next to her.

The prisoners were silent for a few minutes and then someone started to cry. As if on cue, all the women joined in the chorus.

Time seemed to stand still for these carloads of starving, lice-infested women. The train stopped many times throughout the journey since military trains had the right-of-way. Sometimes they waited for days on sidelines not knowing when the train would begin to move again. On those days the doors would be opened for the bodies of the deceased to be removed and, if available, water and straw were replaced. On days when there was soup and bread, everyone was provided their share. Often a few days went by before the women were fed.

Eventually, the prisoners reached their destination of Pocma Mardowska quite a distance past Orszy. Before they reached their designated destination, the elderly and sickly women died and their bodies were thrown from the cars when the trains slowed down to let military transports proceed on the rails. Sometimes, if they passed a village, the townspeople gathered the bodies into wagons and then buried them in mass graves along the tracks. Maria, at first, was despondent when someone died; eventually, she became numb to the horror surrounding her daily. Like everyone with her, Maria only had two thoughts that ran through her brain – food and family. Almost three months had passed during this horrible part of the journey; nonetheless, this would only be the beginning of Maria's ordeal.

Maria believed that Jozef was alive and being the resourceful man he was, he might survive. But all she imagined as the train forged ahead was the sound of the wheels repeating, "Children, children, children."

Maria asked Anna often, "Do you think my girls are alive? Maybe a bomb hit the house. Could they be starving or injured?"

Anna only replied, "Have hope and pray. They are with your parents and other relatives. God willing they will survive this horrible war."

The train finally spit out its remaining passengers at Pocma Mardowska, a labor camp. In this desolate region, the women worked hard in order to get their ration of 500 grams of black, often moldy bread and some boiled soup. Maria had to cut trees, to be used for lumber, from morning until night with only a brief break for lunch. The black bread had to last the whole day; therefore, she and the other women learned to eat small amounts at a time.

After a few weeks, Maria was told that she would no longer cut timber, instead she would be sewing clothing for Soviet soldiers. She knew how to loom flax into linen fabric from her past life on the farm; however, once the material was made a local seamstress came to the farm and made shirts, blouses, skirts, slacks and undergarments for the family. Now, in the span of five days, she was forced to learn how to sew garments for the military or return to the forest to cut trees. Returning to the forest in the sub-zero weather was not an option in her mind. Therefore, she decided to learn how to sew and consequently, receive her allotted rations. A short time later she also had to knit gloves for the Soviet Army, another skill foreign to her but which she learned quickly in order to eat. Her daily quota for glove knitting was 400 grams of bread, which was just enough to survive, and boiled fish bouillon. To add to the insult, the ration of bread was decreased since it was deemed by the commandant of this camp that knitting gloves, albeit thirteen gloves daily, was not as strenuous as chopping trees.

Maria observed the women around her in this dirty, muddy, mosquito infested camp and thought to herself, "We walk like shadows. Our dresses flow on our bodies like gauzy tents since everyone is so emaciated." She could not reconcile in her mind how human beings could treat their fellow humans so cruelly.

Lucky were the few who somehow contacted their families, usually by bribing the guards, and consequently received parcels of food and clothing. Some women shared their good fortune. However, most hoarded their rations for the future since no one knew if their family would survive the war or even send more food. Besides, who knew where they would be sent to next or if they would survive the freezing Russian winters and the diseases that plagued the camps.

Because so many women were dying of dysentery and other diseases, those who had manned the sewing machines or who knitted gloves were again needed to cut timber. Maria was forced to return to the forest to hack away at huge trees and limbs.

One day while out in the frozen woods, a prisoner whose name Maria thought was Zofia, started yelling and screaming at a middle-aged Jewish woman, also a prisoner. Maria met the Jewish lady in a previous prison and according to prison gossip learned that she was a doctor from Wilno.

The doctor was a shy, quiet woman who kept to herself, but this particular day Zofia started screaming at her saying, "It's because of the Jews we are all here. If Hitler hadn't gone after your kind, there would have been no war, no Stalin to arrest us, no horrible camps." With that, Zofia rushed toward the doctor with an axe and was about to strike the frightened woman when Maria grabbed the tool from her screaming out, "What are you doing? Have you gone mad from hunger? This woman is as innocent as we all are and we have to help each other and not kill fellow prisoners. Disease and the Soviets will be more than happy to let us all die. So get back to work before we are all punished for what you almost did." Maria's courage came from a place she forgot existed, but in her heart she knew that she had done the right thing.

With that reprimand, Zofia returned to chopping branches and the doctor thanked Maria for saving her life.

"If ever in my life I can help you Maria, I will. You are a good woman," said the still shaking physician.

"I have nothing against you doctor, or any Jew here. I don't know about Hitler's obsession with your race or with politics in general. But fate brought us to this hell and we must survive. I want to see my girls and husband and I'm sure you have someone you left behind. We must pray that they are all alive and well."

But fate would deal both women a different hand of cards which they would not know about for many months.

In November of 1942, Maria was transported to a camp in Buzuluk and then another in Tashkent in Uzbekstan across the Amu Dar'Ya River. This camp was not any better than the previous ones, but here she came across a friend from a neighboring village, Helena Dulko.

"Maria is that you? You're so skinny and frail!" exclaimed Helena as she hugged her friend through her tears. Maria too was weeping for joy at seeing her former neighbor.

The two women asked each other numerous questions about home, family, arrest, prison camps, etc. Helena explained that she was forcibly dragged from her home in the middle of the night. She begged and pleaded not to be arrested since she was a recent widow whose husband was murdered by bandits and she had five young children, the baby being only nine months old. But she was ripped from the clutching hands of her sons and daughters and yanked away screaming and sobbing.

"I don't know how my family will survive Maria, but I hope and pray daily that they will," uttered the anguished woman.

"But at least we have each other now, Helena, and we can talk about our homes and children," responded Maria. They hugged and cried some more and continued as companions on this journey where they experienced various situations.

Maria and Helena, along with hundreds of other women, traveled on the Amu Dar'Ya River by open barges for five days. Sometimes there was bread, sometimes not, but they finally arrived at another labor camp.

At this God-forsaken camp, the prisoners labored in the fields picking cotton to fulfill their daily quota. The work was intense and the temperature was the opposite of Siberia where they froze. Now women were dying of sunstroke, hunger and typhoid epidemics. The children who survived Siberia's freezing temperatures, succumbed in the heat most readily.

For some unknown reason, after one week, everyone was transported from this labor camp by river barges across the same river to another labor camp. The living conditions were horrible, worse than in previous camps, but they had to remain here for three months. The women, about twenty-five of them, along with children who survived in other camps, lived in a small hut meant for six to ten people. They slept one next to the other as lice marched from person to person nonstop. The stench from dysentery, unwashed bodies, and excrement in the filthy corner bucket was beyond description. It took a long time to get used to labor-camp life. The conditions were unbearable. It was freezing at night, constantly raining, and the women had no choice but to sleep on the bare ground with little clothing and thread-bear, moldy blankets.

"When will they feed us?" an older woman asked as if Maria would have an answer.

"Who knows," was all she could respond.

Food arrived but not in the form of bread. Each woman and child was allotted 400 grams of grain. They had to pound the grain between stones, add water, and cook the flat pancakes over a fire on a flat piece of stone the local peasants provided. Otherwise, they would just eat the grain and swallow it down with water. Sometimes they thought it would be more merciful to be shot, but bullets were saved for the war effort to fight the Germans and these people were expendable since new prisoners arrived daily.

"Helena, it's Christmas Eve," mentioned Maria to her friend. "Why don't we organize a meager meal with the other women in our hut?" she commented.

So they did. Everyone took out a tiny piece of flat bread and passed it around the hut in the old Polish tradition of sharing "The Oplatek," (The Christmas Wafer), symbolic of the presence of Christ, the newborn Child. They hugged and wished each other God's blessings and good health. The war-weary women started singing a Christmas carol, but the atmosphere was as somber as at a funeral, and soon everyone was weeping. Through their tears, they spoke of their lives and their families back home and wondered when this agony would end.

"When will we return to Poland, to our homes?" a young, shivering women asked, not expecting a reply from anyone.

All reminisced about the past and no one had any concrete information. Maria's mind returned to her childhood for a brief moment. "Tata, may I have some hot tea?" she recalled asking her father one Christmas Eve. She loved watching him pour tea so proudly from the silver samovar in their dining area. It stood on the side table in all its glistening glory as her father poured the hot beverage into her teacup. Her family was the only one in the village to have this beautiful tea server and she was delighted to drink her tea feeling so special at that moment. Now, here she was living in prison squalor with only a memory of the taste of tea.

General Anders' Polish Army

Chapter Eleven

One day, sometime around April, 1943, the women got hold of an Uzbek's newspaper which was translated for them by one of the prisoners from another hut. They discovered that an agreement had been reached between the Polish government in exile in England, the United States, and the Soviet Union to free all Polish prisoners, so that they could help the Soviets fight the Germans who had attacked Russia in defiance of their earlier pact.

Within a few weeks of learning this information, Maria and her fellow prisoners were rounded up in the center of the camp. The camp commander showed them a map of Russia and told them where they were at this time. They were told they were free to leave and would be given fifty rubles (Soviet monetary units) each for their journey, along with a small loaf of bread. If they wished to remain or be moved to another part of the USSR, they would get more rubles and new clothes and supposedly plenty to eat.

"Helena, I'm taking the fifty rubles and I will try my luck traveling in the direction of Europe. I've had enough

Soviet hospitality!" uttered Maria.

"I'm going with you," voiced Helena.

The two women, along with many others, but not all since some chose to remain, not trusting the news or the Russians, started out on foot toward Jeozkirta, as suggested by the camp commander. But instead of travelling there, and upon hearing rumors from others on this journey, they arrived in a town called Gruzajewsk and from there continued on to Saransk. According to the rumors, a Polish Army was being organized in this distant city under the auspices of the British Government.

They were in Saransk for three days. Unfortunately, transportation was not available out of there, as they were originally informed. Therefore, they returned to Gruzajewsk where they ran out of food and money.

One night the two women crept into a chicken coop of an Arab family and stole a chicken. They ran a distance away with the squawking bird under Maria's prison jacket and quickly wrung the fowl's neck. They cooked the bird in their one pot, which Maria salvaged from a previous prison, after boiling off the feathers with water from the river. The chicken was eaten a little at a time since golden opportunities like this one did not come along often.

"I feel so guilty about stealing the chicken," Maria confessed to her friend.

"Don't worry," Helena replied, "God will understand."

But months later upon meeting a priest, Maria confessed her sin.

"God forgives you my child since some former prisoners and I also once stole a donkey which we butchered to feed many women and children who were starving. Our prison and post-prison years were horrible and we all did our best to survive and help our fellow prisoners," he stated.

Lacking food or money, the two women asked a passing Uzbek traveler where they could work before continuing on their journey. He pointed them in the direction of a local settlement where an Uzbek farmer might hire them. Maria and Helena proceeded to the group of mud huts covered with straw and the farmer hired them to pick cotton. In exchange, they would be given food and a place to sleep. The old farmer and his wife invited them to stay in their hut until another dwelling could be provided. In the evening, after a hard day of laboring in the hot sun, the farmer's wife asked them to sit on the hardened earth floor and eat with the family. Food consisted of flat unleavened bread which they dipped into a communal pot in the center of the group which contained a soupy consistency of mutton stew. The family was poor, but willing to share what they had with the two women.

Almost two weeks later, Maria and her companion, were told they could move into a tiny mud hut near the farmer's house. Though cramped and dirty, they were satisfied with this since it provided privacy. The tiny hut had no window and only a burlap cloth covered the door. The only light came from a small oil lamp the farmer provided. Their thread-bare blankets were the ones each woman had in her prison cell, but they had to suffice. They tied down the burlap which covered the door with ropes at night, in case anyone tried to enter while they slept. It didn't provide safety, but it might serve as a warning.

One night as they slept, something unusual awoke both women and a terrible fear enshrouded them.

"Maria, what was that?" screamed Helena fearfully.

"I don't know. I felt a strong, cold wind blowing in here and a heavy weight on my body," exclaimed Maria.

"I did too. I couldn't move until it passed. I finally jumped up startled and you did too at the same time."

"What do you think it was?"

"I guess just the wind and our imaginations!"

A few nights later the same situation occurred and the frightened women decided they had had enough. They left the farmer the next day and both believed it was an evil spirit, having been seeped in superstitious tales during their youth.

As they left the Uzbek farm, they started walking toward Gruzajewsk again. They walked for a few hours, exhausted from the heat, when they spotted a man on the roadway ahead of them walking all alone.

"Mister, who are you and where are you going?" they questioned the poor, bedraggled man.

"I'm a freed Polish prisoner and I'm headed to Guzar because I've heard there are people there who are organizing former prisoners and aiding them in joining the Polish Army. I don't know if it's true since rumors are rampant, but you two can join me along my trek."

Helena and Maria listened to this pitiful man describe how horrible his existence had been in the work camps and they, in turn, related their own experiences. When they arrived at the rail line all the train cars were full of passengers. The only transportation available was aboard a flatbed railcar. Therefore, they jumped onto the flatbed car, along with other male and female former prisoners, and headed for Guzar.

"Has anyone here come across a prisoner from the Wilno region names Jozef Pawlukiewicz?" Maria asked those with whom she travelled. No one on this transport had, so she was hopeful her husband was still alive since she had no indication that he had died in the slave labor camps.

At one point, the train stopped at a railroad station and Maria and Helena jumped off the rail car to look for food to purchase from the local Arab's living there. As fate would have it, they became separated. When Maria returned to the spot where she left the train, to her shock, it had departed, along with her friend. She waited overnight for the next train and when it arrived she joined another group of starving, emaciated former prisoners.

During this part of the journey, Maria became extremely ill with dysentery. A man, a total stranger, whose name she never knew, took care of her and saved her life by giving her water and some of his bread. Many people died during this journey to Guzar and were simply wrapped in their old blankets and thrown off the train. At first it was difficult to watch, but eventually, after so many deaths, it was simply accepted as a result of their current situation. Emotions and feelings became a memory of a past existence.

The arrival in Guzar was a shock to Maria and her friend. Before them was a sea of bedraggled humanity. Thousands of former prisoners were waiting in long lines to be examined, fed, and depending on their age and physical condition, accepted into the army. Women with children and hundreds of orphans were moved to other towns in Iran, Africa, or India. Unfortunately, many children died of starvation and illnesses before being shipped to various British colonies.

It was here in Guzar that Maria came across her friend, Helena, who arrived a few days prior. Both women were ecstatic about their reunion. Within a short time their old clothing from prison days was confiscated, they were deloused, provided with clean clothing and awaited further instructions as to when they could enter the Polish Army's branch for women.

After passing the medical commission, Maria was given a uniform and other military equipment and was now a part of the Polish Army. Her first task was working in the army kitchen in twenty-four hour shifts since three thousand soldiers, male and female, had to be fed. The labor was intensive, but finally edible, nutritious food was provided for everyone. Helena also entered the Army and was sent for training to drive convoy trucks. The two friends parted tearfully promising to keep in contact, which they did for many years.

Unfortunately, a terrible typhus epidemic hit the Guzar camp with forty people dying daily. Over three thousand soldiers and civilians died in a six month time period. Maria contracted the awful disease and fortunately was one of the survivors.

One day, as she was returning to her tent from the kitchen, Maria encountered a fellow villager, Mr. Latyszowicz, and inquired about knowledge of her husband and family.

"Prior to my arrest, I know your children were with your parents and when food was scarce, they were taken in by your husband's family. When things got worse there, they returned to your parents. They were like vagabonds, but safe and in good hands," he reinforced. "As to Jozef, I have no knowledge. But hopefully he will turn up soon," he reassured Maria.

Chapter Twelve

On the 10th of May, 1943 , a Polish Military swearing in ceremony was conducted in Guzar at which Maria was a participant. She was now an official member of the Polish Auxilliary Women's Service (PSK) or "Ochotniczki" as they were called. These women soldiers formed an important part of Anders' Army working in kitchens, hospitals, transportation, military offices, or wherever they were needed.

While in Guzar, the Polish Army was visited by General Bohusz-Szyszko, General Wladyslaw Anders, and Bishop Gawlina. General Anders spoke to the soldiers and informed them that in a few days they would be moved across the border and that their horrid suffering would end. For these terribly mistreated former prisoners, this news was the luck they hoped would arrive. They cheered General Anders' speech since he too had survived the same ordeal they had. He was tortured while imprisoned in Moscow's infamous Lubyanka prison; however, Stalin freed him because he needed Anders to organize the Polish Army to fight Germany. Unbeknownst to these men and women, Anders refused to allow Stalin to move these soldiers to the Russian border where Stalin wanted them to fight alongside Soviet soldiers. Instead, he and the British Military personnel convinced Stalin that this newly formed Army should travel through Egypt and Italy and defeat Germany from the South of Europe. Had these men been forced to fight on the Russian front ahead of the Soviets, many who had survived the Siberian labor camps would have died at the Russian border. Stalin considered these people, who were his former prisoners, to be expendable. History later showed, when it was proven that the Soviets rounded up and shot over three thousand Polish officers in the Katyn forest of Poland, how Stalin treated his prisoners. General Anders' wisdom, in not trusting Stalin, saved the lives of many thousands of these newly freed masses.

Life in the army camp became routine for Maria and the rest of the women. Morning exercise, training in military weapons, continued work in the kitchen, and inquiries with the men she met as to her husband's whereabouts. Slowly, mostly due to regular meals, Maria gained weight and started to rebound from starvation. The British provided as much food as necessary for these wretched former prisoners.

Female military personnel who were single, and even some who were married, but had no idea about the survival of their mates, started to socialize with their male counterparts.

Maria was also approached by a Polish Lieutenant.

"Can I walk you to your tent?" suggested the officer.

"If you wish, but I am telling you now that I am devoted to my husband and daughters. I'm not looking for temporary companionship. Besides, there are plenty of young single women here you can get to know better," she responded.

"First of all, I am interested in you and not anyone else here. Secondly, you haven't found your husband yet and there is the possibility that he died in Russia," countered the handsome soldier.

"You are correct in what you say about my Jozef; however, you survived. He is only thirty-five and he was always a strong and resourceful man hence I believe he is alive and trying to get here. If by the end of this war he does not return, you can contact me and we can discuss the future then. And keep in mind I have children and I want to return to them and my family," Maria responded strongly and sincerely.

"You are an amazing woman and I greatly admire you. We shall see how our lives continue, but I am fond of you," he said smiling.

"I appreciate your kind words but I still believe you should approach the single women here. There is a wonderful young woman residing in my tent and if you wish I will introduce her to you. Think about it and please realize I am serious in what I have said to you," commented Maria, "And thank you for walking me to my tent."

"My pleasure and honor," responded the Lieutenant as he kissed her hand in the Polish custom.

Finally, on August 11th, the transport trains arrived in Guzar Valley to move the Polish Army toward Baghdad. The horrible tragedy was that after surviving the cold of Siberia and the unrelenting heat of the Kazakstan and Uzbekstan deserts, many thousands died in this region which was supposed to be their salvation. But disease doesn't care who you are or what you went through; it sweeps its mighty hand over all and points its fingers at the next victim. The hope of returning to Poland would never be the reality of those buried here and across all of Russia.

The transport arrived in Krasnovodsk on the 13th of August and remained there for three days. For some unknown reason, water was non-existent and thousands of people began to suffer in the extreme heat. Maria became ill from dehydration and was taken off the train by stretcher to a field hospital where she recovered and was then brought back to her travel companions.

On the 19th of August, the trains arrived at the seaport town of Pahlavi in Persia. The Caspian Sea was enticing so Maria and some of the women bathed in the refreshing waters.

"Isn't this grand," one of the women exclaimed. After being held in such filth and squalor in Uzbekstan, the waters from this sea were like a baptism into a new life.

"I've never seen such a huge body of water. In our village in Poland, we had a river and lakes, but nothing compared to this," explained the excited Maria. "I can't wait to share this experience with my children. They'll think I'm making up fairy tales like I did when they were little." Maria had a talent for telling stories to her daughters. Before they fell asleep, her girls were regaled with tales of magical bears living in caves filled with toys and cakes and unbelievably beautiful dresses. She hoped to continue her stories when they were a family again.

Unfortunately, Maria's adventure in the Caspian Sea led to a bout of malaria. She was hospitalized for two weeks with hundreds of other malaria patients. Luckily, she recovered and felt very well since the treatment and quality of care provided by the British doctors and nurses was quite good. Once she recuperated, she was transferred, along with the others who recovered, to a hospital in Teheran just to be sure she was well enough for active duty. After a one week stay in the hospital ward, she was assigned to the 4th Army Military Camp in Kanakin. Her time there was brief and she was again transported to a military camp in Kizil–Ribot. In March of 1944, Maria was assigned to Baghdad where she continued her work in the camp kitchen.

Baghdad, in the mid 1940's, was a beautiful city. Certainly, it was like nothing Maria had seen in her Polish village of Zoltuny, or in the city of Wilno, for that matter. Granted, Wilno had its stone mansions, market squares, a university, and many impressive churches. Our Lady of Ostrabrama Church was Maria's favorite and she visited there whenever Jozef went to Wilno to sell farm produce, rye, oats, or wheat. Nevertheless, Baghdad was unique with its mosaic tile work, minarets, and exotic markets selling fruits and vegetables she had never seen before and fabrics that glistened like jewels in the hot sun.

While stationed in Baghdad, Maria became friends with the head cook in the military kitchen. He was an older man, in his fifties, and wasn't accepted to serve in the Polish Army due to age and medical issues acquired from his Siberian imprisonment. Instead, he was assigned the task of camp cook. All military personnel were provided with cigarettes, chocolate, and other necessary personal items from the British government so he and Maria decided to form a business partnership. They sold or bartered these goods with the local Arabs for leather. They then sold the leather to shoemakers in the city and made some money. The cook even traded potato peels for a leather belt he needed. People were very poor in this region of the world; therefore, they were willing to sell or trade almost anything. One time, Maria found a burlap bag alongside the road and bartered it for a small carved ivory fish that caught her eye. She thought that one day she might sell it since all the money she made in her dealings she saved believing that eventually, she would be able to send it to her family for their needs in war-torn Poland.

Adventures in this city continued for Maria and a few companions when, one day while on leave, they ventured into Baghdad to stroll through the various outdoor markets.

The various scented oils and colorful cloths enticed these Polish women since they were not familiar with these unique items in Poland. Unfortunately, they still had very little money so purchasing these edible delicacies, enticing perfumes, or silky fabrics was out of the question.

"Maria I think we're lost," stated Genia as they traversed the alleyways between markets.

"Let's stay together and try to find our way to the main road," replied Stefania.

As they continued on they entered a large courtyard with close to fifty Arab men sitting around the perimeter and talking loudly and laughing in small clusters. Suddenly, a hush fell over the crowd as a line of women and girls was brought to the center of the courtyard.

"What do you think is going on?" wondered Stefania out loud.

"I don't know, but I think we'll soon see," replied Maria.

Within a few minutes a few men from the periphery stepped forward, walked up to each woman, lifted her veil, examined her teeth, felt her breasts and made a monetary offer.

"My God, they're buying wives! How barbaric! Let's get away from here. I'm afraid it might be dangerous to stay," exclaimed Maria as they headed back to their camp.

The women were in shock since they were totally

unfamiliar with such practices. In Poland, when a girl was of age to marry, young men came courting. The girl's father stated the dowry, and arrangements were made for the ceremony. Very rarely did the father force a daughter to marry someone she didn't know or at least like. Polish countryside marriages were usually made to join lands and increase property size. But the sale of these young Arab women, some as young as ten, left the Polish Military women visibly shaken especially because some of these girls were the ages of their own daughters forcibly left back home.

Chapter Twelve

Maria became seriously ill in Baghdad and was scheduled to undergo surgery for a feminine issue which in those years was not discussed. She was taken to the Third Army Hospital in Kizil-Ribot. Just before Maria's surgery, her commanding officer requested that she report to headquarters immediately.

"I wonder what she wants from me. Maybe my surgery is being postponed," Maria stated to her tent-mates.

"Don't worry Maria, she's probably giving you a raise!" laughed one of the women in the tent.

Maria adjusted her uniform, wiped the dust from her shoes, combed her now short hair and walked briskly to the Captain's tent. She presented herself to the Captain's secretary and was led down the hall of a large tent. She was getting nervous not knowing what to expect.

The flaps of the tent door opened to reveal the Captain sitting at her desk and facing Maria. Maria saluted saying, "Ochotniczka (voluntary soldier) Maria Pawlukiewicz reporting." Just at that moment, which was only seconds, she saw the back of the head of a male soldier sitting directly in front of her.

"Jozef!" she screamed as she realized that it was her husband. Without asking permission, she rushed toward him, and wrapped her arms around him while sobbing and trembling all at once. Through their tears, they clung to each other fearful of another separation.

"I believe you two can be dismissed. So find a place to talk and reunite," remarked the Captain with a broad smile on her face.

It seems that as Maria was inquiring in every camp about Jozef, he was doing the same. He finally learned that she was in Baghdad and he received a two day leave to find his long lost wife. After exiting the Captain's quarters, the couple climbed a small hill, sat on the dry desert grass and began to discuss their unspeakable experiences.

"Do you know anything about our daughters Jozef?" Maria queried her recently discovered husband after telling him what she had learned from their former neighbor, Mr. Latyszowicz.

"I tried to get information," he responded as he dried his tears, "but I know nothing. Maybe this war will be over soon and we can return home. Just pray Maria that neither of us will be killed."

"What have you been assigned to Jozef?" she asked.

"I'm in the Polish II Corps of the Sapper Division of the Third Carpathian Brigade. As far as I know, I'll be building roads and bridges to transport soldiers and equipment through the various embattled area of North Africa and eventually Europe. But my commanding officer wants me to be trained to diffuse land mines. He says I'm calm and quick and could do the job. Truthfully, I don't care what my assignment will be; I just want all this to end as quickly as possible."

"Where did they take you in Russia?" was her next question to her labor-camp weary husband.

"They kept changing our camps, but I was close to the Mongolian border in the areas of Novosibirsk, Tomsk, and Krasnoyarsk. I don't have to tell you how dreadfully difficult it was to survive, but I made it. Sometimes I was so hungry, I ate any grass I could find and even tree bark. They worked us hard to make our daily quota and many men died, especially those from the cities who had desk jobs. Those among us who were farmers, factory workers, masons, and carpenters did better, but it was still an experience defying description. In the summers, the ground was pure mud. Flies, gnats, and mosquitoes were everywhere. In the winter months, we froze. So many men lost fingers and toes to frostbite and even nose tips and ear lobes froze and fell off. I still have the feeling of constant cold and tingling in the heels of my feet."

"There was no point in forming lasting friendships because you didn't know whom to trust or who would be dead that night or in the morning. And besides, some of the men were criminals and you had to watch your back constantly. A hierarchy existed in the penal system and criminals often had more power than the guards. Murder was common, as was homosexuality, but fortunately, I was never approached. I tried to share my meager rations with everyone – the worst and the best, so as not to become a target," stated Jozef matter-of-factly to his wife. "But we pushed on, Maria, and cut timber and used the logs to build roads and bridges. We prayed silently for God to find us in that desolate wilderness and get us out. And He did, and thankfully, I found you. Now we can at least keep in touch and we might even be able to get leave time together," remarked the dejected, albeit now free man, since he knew that other dangers awaited him and his fellow soldiers.

"Jozef, I can't believe two and a half years have gone by. I thought I might never see you again. I am so fortunate that God heard my prayers," and Maria burst into tears again. Their visit was brief but they never stopped talking and crying.

After Jozef left, Maria underwent surgery and spent that Easter in the hospital. Once she left the hospital, she was sent to a convalescent home in Baghdad for the next eighteen days. She was then assigned to the First Army Hospital in Kirkuk to again work in the kitchen. It was here that she accidentally ran into the Jewish doctor whose life she saved in one of the labor camps.

Maria was covering her friend's shift in the hospital changing sheets, washing them, scrubbing floors and removing chamber pots – whatever was requested of her, when the doctor spotted her.

"Maria, is it you? You look so much better than the last time I saw you!"

"Doctor, you survived!" Maria exclaimed.

"Maria I can't believe they have you doing such menial tasks. You're too intelligent for this hard labor. Let me speak to the hospital director. I can train you for more worthwhile work in this hospital. Besides, I owe you so much for saving my life in that freezing forest."

"Thank you doctor. I'll do anything asked of me. I'm just so glad to be out of the labor camps and all that horror," remarked Maria as she took up the mop and pail.

The doctor was true to her word and Maria was sent for training to be a nurse's aide. Her tasks now included changing dressings, dispensing medications, keeping records, taking temperatures and uplifting the spirits of so many war-damaged patients. Eventually, when the field hospital was moved closer to the war zone, just behind the military lines, Maria helped care for innumerable wounded soldiers. But that was still some time away.

While they were both in the area of Baghdad, Jozef and Maria met when they could get a day of leave time. On one of these days, Maria asked Jozef to accompany her to a dentist since she was experiencing a toothache. When they arrived at the Arab dentist's office, he escorted Maria into the inner room and locked the door. Jozef was asked to wait in the reception area. Maria started to feel uncomfortable as the dentist started to make inappropriate advances to her. She started to jesture that her husband was outside the door and that once he took care of her tooth, she would return alone. This seemed to please him and he treated her aching tooth.

"Jozef, let's get out of here as quickly as possible!" she exclaimed excitedly.

"What's wrong, what happened in there?" he questioned.

After she explained what had happened Jozef wanted to return and accost the dentist, but Maria prevented him.

"We don't know if he has friends there and you could be killed. We're not going back!" she stated emphatically.

"These people have a different culture and belief than we do and they have no respect for women. I've heard of women who were abducted into harems and couldn't leave or they would be killed. I saw with my own eyes how an Arab threw a knife into his wife's back while she was carrying their toddler. He killed her because her eyes strayed from beneath her veil at another man. Let's get back to our camp and avoid problems," the shaky woman uttered.

In the month of September, all army hospital personnel were notified that they would be transferred from Kirkuk to Palestine. Once in Palestine, Maria procured an eight day leave and she used those days to visit Jozef at his army camp. On one particular day, Jozef surprised his wife.

"Maria let's go visit the church in the spot where Christ was buried in Jerusalem. There's a group of us going along with a priest as guide. We may never be in this part of the world again and I want to see this sacred spot and thank God for saving us." However, Jozef had a second motive that he saved for the right moment.

After they visited the Church of the Holy Sepulcher, and when everyone left, except Maria and her husband, Jozef asked the priest, "Father, can we renew our wedding vows here?"

"Of course," replied the prelate.

Jozef then produced two gold wedding bands which he bought with money he saved from his small army pay. Their original bands were taken by the Soviets long ago. Once the priest blessed the new wedding rings, Maria placed one on her husband's finger and he reciprocated. They repeated their vows pledging to love and cherish each other forever. Maria cried and Jozef wiped away her tears and consoled her as best he could in this holy place.

After their sojourn to Palestine, the First Army Hospital was transferred to Quantara in Egypt. Jozef was still in Palestine, but on her next leave from the hospital, Maria received word that the Polish Army was being boarded onto transport ships in Port Said and Cairo, Egypt and sent to Taranto, Italy where the soldiers were needed to fight the Germans.

Soon thereafter, Maria and the field hospital would also be transported to Italy because the battles against the German Army were expected to be intense and the casualties many.

Under the command of Lieutenant General Wladyslaw

Anders, the Third Carpathian Division, Polish II Corps was united with the British Eighth Army under General Oliver Leese. The two armies joined the American Army in the various battles in Italy. Jozef was a Corporal in the Sapper Division of the army and eventually attained the rank of Sergeant. They fought the Germans in cities such as Bologna, Ancona, Loreto, Casa Massima, and most importantly, in Monte Cassino. It was here that fifty thousand Polish soldiers were dispatched to conquer the German stronghold at this mountain-top monastery. The battle ensued on May 12th, 1944 and ended May 19th when the Polish soldiers successfully defeated the Germans entrenched there. Unable to find a Polish flag, the 12th Podalski Lancers Regiment constructed a flag from parts of a Red Cross flag and a blue handkerchief and hung it atop the ruins of the abbey on a tree limb. The "Krakow Hejnal," a medieval Polish military signal, was sounded on the bugle of Section Leader Czeh and heard loudly from the monastery hill.

This horrid battle of Monte Cassino ended with the Germans surrendering. In order to accomplish this feat, which the other Allied armies could not do, four thousand Polish soldiers gave their lives. Fortunately, Jozef and his comrades survived and continued fighting toward Rome. Jozef's steady hands and calm disposition caused his commanding officers to place the newly minted Sergeant as leader of his men in finding and disarming land mines prior to the approach of the rest of the combatants. Through luck and skill, Jozef survived this task without a physical scratch. Unfortunately, psychological scars manifested themselves in his later years with a low tolerance toward alcohol – his poison of choice. Although he was not one to discuss the maiming or death of his friends, the experiences of war taxed the psyche of many soldiers, even Jozef. Watching fellow prisoners die by the hundreds in Siberia and then to see comrades-in-arms perish or be maimed in Italy was disastrous for even the most courageous of men. But he was a survivor and did his utmost to prove himself in battle and was awarded numerous medals for his loyal service.

Maria fought her own battle as a nurse's aide during the Italian offensive. She saw soldier after soldier destroyed by war's weaponry as they were brought to the field hospital in various stages of agony due to their severe wounds.

Maria remembered one young soldier in particular. This severely injured man often begged for her assistance.

"Nurse, nurse, please help me," was a constant call from this young warrior.

"Nurse, please can you light a cigarette for me," pleaded the young blue-eyed corporal. He was suspended in a hammock above his bed while his sheets were being changed.

"You know I can't corporal. I have so many soldiers to tend to and holding your cigarette as you smoke is not possible at the moment. Surely, later I will return," replied Maria as she gathered his sheets.

"But if you light it, I can smoke it without bothering you," again the corporal begged.

"I promise, I'll return as soon as I finish my tasks," was her sincere reply.

But Maria knew the corporal's mission was self-immolation since he begged the doctors daily to end his life. The poor soul lost both arms and legs and only a torso and head swung in the hammock. Maria couldn't even imagine what his life would be like in the future; fortunately, she didn't need to worry. Infection set in, and the blue-eye soldier passed.

The battle in Italy continued until Rome was liberated. Military leaves were out of the question during this phase of the war, but Maria continued to communicate with her husband through numerous letters. There was no actual mail service, but whenever a convoy of ammunition or supplies was being moved toward the battlefields, Maria handed a letter to one of the drivers.

"Please, if you get near soldiers from the Carpathian Brigade, give this to someone who can pass it on to my husband," her pleading blue-eyes requested.

"Absolutely. I'll do my best," the soldier promised.

Some mail reached its destination, some, of course, never did due to a myriad of reasons. Usually, Jozef could not be located since he and his men were in some war-torn village or isolated mountain road. But when he was fortunate enough to receive a letter, Jozef rejoiced that his wife was still alive.

Eventually, the Germans were defeated in Italy and the war-weary couple was granted leave from their duties. They tried to plan leaves at the same time but this was no easy matter. Both were needed in their respective military positions.

On one occasion, just prior to the end of the war, they met in Bari, Italy where Maria rented a small back room from an Italian carpenter and his wife. Guiseppe and his wife, Maria, had two daughters they fiercely protected from military personnel in the area. Word had gotten to them that not all soldiers who were part of the British Eighth Army were noble, virtuous men. The Arab soldiers from North Africa were rumored to have ravaged females in many towns in Italy, and Guiseppe kept his daughters from their view. But he took a liking to this Polish couple and rented his room so they could have a bit of privacy and peace. He was so fond of Maria that he even made her a lovely wooden box where she could store her few worldly possessions. In later years, it was placed on top of her dresser where family and friends could admire the intricate carvings. Maria cared for this treasure not because it held her trinkets, but because it held so many memories of her war-life.

Since the couple could only see each other three to four times a year, they cherished their moments. They shared thoughts about their terrible incarceration, the constant hunger pangs, and daily fear from their jailers. During one rendezvous, Jozef told Maria about a highly dangerous plan he was formulating.

In late winter and early spring of 1945, when rumors among the military personnel started swirling throughout the army camps that Germany would soon surrender, Jozef came upon three Polish civilians, part of the Polish underground, who had made plans with a few of his fellow soldiers. The secretive plans entailed entering Poland clandestinely and kidnapping children left behind due to the war situation, and smuggling them across the various borders to their respective parents in Italy.

"Maria, they want money to get our children. I have some saved and my friends have agreed to lend me what they can to help us out," stated Jozef excitedly.

"I have some money also. I sold some leather to an Italian shoe-maker which I bought cheaply in Palestine. And maybe some of my friends could also lend me money. I made a feather comforter for an Italian lady and she said her friends need them also. All I need is down and fabric and I can sew them like I did in Poland. We'll raise as much money as we can as long as we can get our girls," exclaimed the hopeful mother through tearful eyes.

When their brief time together was over, Maria and her husband returned to their respective military camps. He continued to lead his men into battle and she continued to aid the wounded and pained.

Jozef met with the three men about a month later, just a few days after Germany surrendered, and they discussed the plan to smuggle Helena and Bronia out of Poland, which was now in Soviet hands. If the men were captured, torture and death would be the result. But they said they had succeeded twice before so everyone was hopeful. After information was provided and money exchanged, the three men set out on their journey.

Weeks went by as Jozef and Maria waited for word about their children. Meantime, with the war's end, Jozef and his men continued to clear roads and bridges of land mines. Civilians started returning home and their safety was of high concern. Rubble was strewn everywhere and before anything could be rebuilt by the local townsmen, live ammunition had to be secured. As he went about this task, Jozef worried about his young daughters and wondered if the men would be able to complete their mission. After all, Wilno was in the Northeast corner of Poland as he knew it at the time, but now it belonged to Lithuania. So the men had to cross the borders of Yugoslavia, Hungary, and Czechoslovakia before entering Southern Poland and continuing on to Wilno, or Vilnius as it was now called. This was a major undertaking for the brave men; hopefully, they would return with the two girls.

"What are you sewing Maria?" Jadzia asked her friend.

"It's an undershirt for my youngest daughter, Bronia. She was a little over three when I was arrested so I'm guessing her size now. I hope it fits since the material was difficult to get, but a kind Italian lady sold me a few yards. I'll make blouses for Helena also. She's almost twelve now, so again I'm guessing as to the fit. But this keeps me occupied, otherwise I just think about my poor girls and cry. Actually, I haven't stopped crying since we were separated," Maria revealed to her friend and fellow soldier-nurse.

Meanwhile, Jozef waited for word about his children's return.

"Sergeant, there are three men outside your tent who want to see you," reported a young-faced private.

Jozef, jumped up, startled from his bunk. His moment of rest ended as he threw on his shirt while tucking it into his pants as he ran out of the tent.

"Sergeant, we've returned, but the news isn't good," said the leader to Jozef.

"Tell me. Are my children alive?" Jozef asked.

"We don't know because we had to abort the mission. It became too dangerous. We got as far as the Polish border but it was too heavily guarded by the Russians and we couldn't get across. We are so sorry, but it was impossible," he continued with sadness in his voice.

He gave the stunned Jozef any money they didn't use for their journey, but it didn't assuage the young father. How would he tell his wife he wondered and when would he see his family united? He cursed the war and the men who started it as he wiped the tears from his eyes, returned to his tent, and sat down to write a difficult letter to his wife.

When Maria received the letter and read its message, she grasped the letter to her heart and sat on her cot shedding copious tears. Her companions tried to console her to no avail.

"Maria, don't despair. We're all being sent to England soon and maybe you can get your girls there somehow," conjectured Zosia one of the fellow nurse's aides.

"No Zosia. Rumors say that the borders will be closed soon and my children will never leave Poland," sobbed Maria.

"No, that cannot be. I need to see my family also," cried Jadwiga.

"Me too," added Klara. "I want to see my parents and sister," she continued through sobs.

Soon everyone was crying about the hopelessness of their situation. Would they ever return home? Who was still alive? Why did this war happen? Why do people have to hate each other? What was the reason for so many dead, wounded, and scarred? But these questions were not new, just asked at a different period in history and no one knew the answer to any of them.

Maria knew one thing. Despite her deep faith and trust in God, she could not understand why she had to lose her daughters a second time. She could not accept that her maker could be so heartless, yet she continued to hope and pray. She had something in her being that refused to let her give up hope.

Great Britain
1945 - 1951

Chapter Thirteen

England was the next phase of the journey for Jozef and his wife. He and all the male soldiers boarded a transport ship in Italy. Meanwhile, she traveled with the women and the war wounded, since the nurse's aides were necessary in caring for the war-mangled men.

While aboard the transport ship, Jozef started to feel ill. He thought he was seasick since he had never travelled on such huge bodies of water as the Mediterranean Sea and the Atlantic Ocean.

"Jozef, what's wrong with you?" questioned Ludwik, his friend and fellow soldier.

"I don't know. I thought this sea voyage was making me ill, but I don't think so," he replied. "I can't seem to move my hands or feet. I need a medic, Ludwik. See if you can find one on board."

Ludwik returned with a male nurse who examined the ailing soldier.

"I'm not a doctor, but this seems like some kind of paralysis. When we get to Southampton, we'll get him off by stretcher and into a military hospital," conveyed the medic.

"But my wife is on another transport ship. Can you get word to her so she can be near me? She is expecting our baby and I can't lose track of her or another child again," Jozef asserted to Ludwik and the medic.

"I will inform your commanding officer Sergeant and I'm sure that he will do his utmost to keep you both in proximity. I haven't found my wife and son since 1940 and I'm sure they perished somewhere in Siberia. We all know what you're experiencing and sympathize. For the time being, try to rest until we arrive in England. Worry and stress can't be good for you in this condition. Let me know if things get worse for you," stated the medic.

The thousands of soldiers and displaced Polish women and children from Africa and India, arrived in England in the mid 1940's. The British set up Displaced Persons (DP) or resettlement camps throughout England, Scotland and Wales. Many of the camps were former RAF air bases. The Poles were housed in Nissen huts which were prefabricated shelters having a semi-circular arching roof made of corrugated iron sheets and set on a concrete floor. There was no running water in these huts, but there were communal water pumps, bathrooms, outhouses, and showers. Living conditions were not the best, especially in winter, but everyone was free from Soviet tyranny and Siberia's hell, so this was luxury living.

As expected, Jozef was taken off the ship by stretcher

since he could not walk or use his hands. He was transported to a hospital near Diddington in Cambridgeshire. Maria was sent to the military hospital in Diddington also, thanks to the help of Jozef's commanding officer.

Here Jozef was under the care of British and Polish doctors who treated him as best they could. No one really diagnosed his condition, but the British doctors ordered constant physical therapy while the Polish doctors recommended vitamin and nutritional therapy. Maria visited her husband daily on her free time since she was still a military nurse's aide and had much work to do with the wounded. But she came to feed Jozef, wash him, shave him, and care for his personal needs while doing her best to cheer him up.

Meanwhile, Maria started to prepare for the birth of her child. She still had the shirts and other clothing she made for her older daughters, so she sat up nights and reworked the garments to fit a newborn. She resided at the Sixth Polish Army Hospital near Diddington Park, since she wanted to be near Jozef. Her quarters were a bunk bed and a military issued trunk where she kept her few belongings. She did not have maternity clothes so she sewed two of her Army uniform skirts together to make one outfit that fit her now expanding body. But she didn't mind as long as she had her husband nearby slowly recovering and a child on the way.

On December 24, 1946, the now thirty-three year old Maria gave birth to a daughter, Irena Maria. It was a long and arduous birth, just like her previous ones and again there was no medication to ease the pain. A nurse stopped by every so often to examine her; however, a midwife delivered the child.

"Notify Jozef that the baby has been born," she requested of her friend and fellow nurse's aide, Jozefa Gawronska.

"Of course Maria, but you know he still can't walk," replied Jozefa.

"I know. But at least he'll know," said the labor-weary mother.

Jozef sent word that he was elated, but couldn't come to see her since it was Christmas and the hospital was understaffed. He came just after the New Year to see his wife and child. Maria was placed on maternity leave for a few months after the birth of her daughter. After this period, she continued her duties in the hospital tending to the Polish wounded soldiers and their families.

In January, the couple had their daughter Christened in the hospital in the presence of the godparents, Jozefa Gawronska and Ludwik Szulc. The parents and guests celebrated the event with a bottle of wine, brought from Italy, bread, pickles, and a can of sardines since food was scarce and rationed in war-torn England. Nevertheless, everyone was pleased, even the priest, since the mother and child were doing well. Jozef's health improved and by late fall of 1947 he and his family were resettled in a Polish camp near Kelvedon, England with hundreds of other former Polish soldiers and their families.

Life was not easy in the resettlement camp, especially for these non-English speaking people. Each family was assigned half of a Nissen hut which the Poles christened, "beczki," or barrels. Each hut was partitioned with a brick wall separating the two occupying families. A wood burning stove was used for heat and cooking, and a wash basin was provided in which water from the outdoor pump was brought in for heating up and then washing. The outhouse was situated in an area where a few families had access. The communal showers were housed in another hut – one for women and children and a separate one for men. There was one drafty window which Maria covered with a blanket during the cold winter months. Maria separated the main part of the hut with blankets, hung on ropes, so that there was some privacy in the sleeping area. As soon as spring came, she started a vegetable garden and Jozef built a small chicken coop since everything was rationed in England after the war. Their three member family simply couldn't improve their health on five eggs per week and a pound of flour and a bit of meat. As Irena grew older, Maria placed her daughter with an older woman in the camp who cared for a few children. Meanwhile, she found work picking crops for various farmers in the vicinity of the camp. Eventually, Jozef recovered from the paralysis of his feet and hands and found work in the construction of roads and bridges.

At Christmas of 1947, the Polish families tried to

celebrate the festive holiday in their homeland's traditions. A Polish priest came to say Mass in one of the Nissen huts as everyone tried to sing Polish carols through their tears. Everyone was affected by the war. Many still had family in Poland or in Polish camps in India, Africa, Mexico, and other parts of the world. Many wives and husbands were unable to leave Russia and were still prisoners. Women who tried to traverse the steps out of prison camps were kept by Asiatic nomads as slaves. Others cried because they lost family members to torture, disease, or starvation. But they sang and prayed believing that they were saved for a reason. No one knew yet what that reason was or where life's journey would take them. Therefore, they continued to keep their Polish holiday traditions alive in remembrance of happier times in their homeland, until the next phase of their lives sent them in another direction.

Just before Christmas, Maria realized that she was pregnant and another child would be born in July of 1948. She and Jozef wrote to their families in Poland as soon as they arrived in England, but did not receive a return message for almost two years. The news was good in that Helena and Bronia were alive as were all the other family members. The children were living with Maria or Jozef's parents depending on who could afford to care for them. Both families lost their farms to the Soviet "kolhoz," or collective farm system, so food was scare and there were many hungry family members. They struggled terribly but survived the terrible post-war years. No possibility existed for the girls to come to England at this time. In addition, their parents could not return to Poland since soldiers who were part of General Anders' Army were immediately sent to Siberia upon returning to Poland on the grounds that they had to complete their original prison sentence. Since Maria and Jozef only served two and a half years of their five years of hard labor sentence, they would be sent back to the depths of Russia to complete the rest of their prison time, or even retried, tortured, or killed.

A good army friend of Jozef's told him that he was returning to his family in Poland.

"Jozef, I will write to you in code. If I tell you that everything is great in Poland, do not return. It will mean the opposite."

He kept his word and the message proved to be sincere since he was arrested, along with his wife and son and sent back to Siberia where he eventually died. This Jozef found out from other former soldiers he met years later who came from the same village.

On July 31st, 1948, Maria gave birth to another daughter, Teresa Veronica. Her friend from Poland, prison, and the army, Helena Dulko, was Teresa's godmother, along with Mr. Chmara, a military friend of Jozef's.

Helena and Maria kept in touch during their army service and after the war Helena was placed in a camp near Kelvedon. The two women experienced similar imprisonment, separation from children, military life, and now life in England. Neither could return to her homeland

and children and each awaited the future with both hope and dread, not trusting any government.

One day, Jozef came home from working on road building and told Maria that General Anders was going to visit their resettlement camp to see for himself how his former soldiers were prospering in England. The following day, one of the camp leaders came to their dwelling to inform the couple that their home was chosen as one of the residences the General would visit.

"Jozef, I have to prepare our home for this visit," stated the nervous Maria.

"Don't worry, our house is neat and clean. If anything, make some tea and bake your delicious "babka", responded Jozef calmly.

The following morning, General Anders, with his military entourage, and his wife, Irena Bogdanska Anders, arrived at Maria and Jozef's Nissen hut. Mrs. Anders was especially happy to see the two little girls who were so neatly dressed for the occasion. They were pleased with what they saw and after a brief stay, and a cup of tea and Maria's cake, they praised the couple and thanked them for their hospitality. The couple was thrilled that their home was chosen for the inspection and spoke of the visit often.

In the late 40's and early 50's, the British government agreed to provide free passage to former Polish soldiers in DP (Displaced Persons) camps if they agreed to leave. They would be provided with transportation to Canada, Argentina, the United States, or could remain in England.

Maria and Jozef had to make a decision soon.

"Jozef, should we stay here?" wondered Maria.

"There is little work here Maria, now that the British soldiers have returned," replied her husband. "We would be struggling a long time before we could afford an apartment or even a home."

"Helena is going to Argentina," she stated.

"I know, but I don't think that's the place for us. Mostly single Polish people are moving there."

"My uncle lived in America in the 1920's," commented Maria. "He returned to Poland in the 1930's and bought land and farmed. But he lost it all now. He spoke well of America. He said if you worked hard you could do well there. Should we go?" she asked.

"I think so. I heard from a friend that after living there five years we could become citizens. Then we could bring our girls to America from Poland."

"Then America it is!"

Complication occurred when Maria was asked to go to the bureau dealing with departures from England. In her military documents, her last name was listed as Pawlukowicz while Jozef was Pawlukiewicz. She realized her error with great embarrassment. It seemed that when she completed her paperwork to enter the Polish Army, she gave her name incorrectly because she was so mentally exhausted and physically ill with the remnants of dysentery. This error followed Maria even to her daughter, Irena's, birth certificate. Therefore, all her documents had to be corroborated by those who knew her from her days in Poland. Jozef too, gave his birth date as February 28th when he entered the military since he forgot the actual date. It wasn't until he received a copy of his Baptismal and birth certificate from his parish in Poland that he remembered the actual date as February 2nd. Their experiences in Siberia caused untold havoc on their memories, but eventually everything was corrected and they could leave England.

The bus arrived at Kelvedon to take the family to Southampton Harbor. They said their goodbye's to their friends who came to see them off on their journey. Maria left a bowl of milk for their adopted cats, since the girls tearfully insisted. A few families would also be leaving soon to settle in Pittsburg, Pennsylvania, New Britain, Connecticut, and Detroit, Michigan. Maria and Jozef were traveling to New York City even though they knew no one there, had no jobs waiting, and spoke no English. It seemed like a dismal undertaking, but after Siberia's prison camps this was an easy challenge.

In Southampton, they boarded the Queen Elizabeth I for the transatlantic voyage. Other than the four-year old Irena, the other family members were quite seasick. A family in the adjacent cabin took the girl with them to mealtimes and she always brought back bread and jam for her sick family, especially her three-year old sister, Teresa.

AMERICA
May 22, 1951

Chapter Fourteen

On May 22nd, the Pawlukiewicz family arrived in New York harbor and disembarked from the beautiful ocean liner. Their one trunk was already waiting for them on the dock. Maria and Jozef each carried suitcases while the girls carried small bags of their own childhood possessions.

"Irena, you and your sister sit on our trunk and watch the suitcases while your father and I find out where we can go from here," were the instructions given the children who dutifully obeyed.

As Maria and her husband walked away from the girls to find information, a woman heard them speaking Polish.

"Are you looking for your family?" she asked in Polish.

"No, we don't know anyone here," they responded in their native tongue.

"I can help you. Let's go back to your children," she stated.

The stranger hired the family a taxi cab and gave the driver instructions to take them to a hotel near St. Mark's Place. She gave them the address of Father Burant, a Polish priest, who might be able to help them.

The family arrived at their designated hotel where they remained for a few days. The day after their arrival, Jozef went to Father Burant with instructions from his wife.

"Tell the priest that we don't want to live in the city. Ask if he can find us work in the country. It would be healthier for the girls to live in the fresh air, with less noise, and a cleaner environment," she stated self-confidently.

Father Burant spoke with Jozef about his previous life and upon assuring himself of Jozef's skills, he told Jozef to return the next day once he made some inquiries.

True to his word, Father Burant told Jozef that he had a position for him just east of Riverhead on Long Island, in Aquebogue. A farmer of Polish decent, Mr. Sawicki, needed workers on his farm. The priest arranged tickets on the Long Island Railroad for the family and the following morning they left New York City for Aquebogue.

Mr. Sawicki gathered the family into his pickup truck from the train station and luckily he spoke Polish. He drove them to his farm and apologized that their living quarters were a rundown shack not far from the impressive two story brick home he and his wife occupied.

After he left them, Maria burst into tears.

"Why did we leave England? At least we knew what we had there and maybe our circumstances would have improved. But we have to live in this hovel, with an outhouse and no running water. And look at the mattresses on the floor – they're filthy! I want to go back!" she sobbed.

"We can't Maria. We don't have the money and we'll do our best here and in time get work elsewhere and leave."

The couple spent the rest of May, June and July working in the hot sun harvesting potatoes, cauliflower, asparagus, and strawberries.

The girls followed them to the fields but also spent time playing with newly hatched chicks, mooing along with the cow, or chasing kittens. They were usually left to their own devices, and being young, were often in trouble. Once, Mrs. Sawicki yelled at them when they washed the farmer's newborn kittens in the tank of kerosene they found on the side of the barn causing all the felines to die. Another time, Maria scolded Irena because she bathed Teresa in an aluminum tub of ice cold water she pumped from the bright red hand pump. By August, Maria had enough and insisted the family move to an apartment in Riverhead.

Their new dwelling, in a three story apartment house, was not first rate since the stairs were rickety and needed repair desperately and the kitchen sink was the only area for running water. The bathtub was down the hall and used by all the apartment occupants on that floor and the outhouse was located behind the one-car garage. But it was better than the farmer's shack and would suffice. Jozef and a couple of male tenants repaired the staircase and the family began the second phase of their American life.

Jozef continued to work for Mr. Sawicki during the day. The farmer picked him up six days a week to do farm labor. For the evening hours, he acquired a job at a bowling alley setting up pins, before mechanization took over. Maria found a job in a local soup canning company shucking clams for clam chowder. The daughters were either on the farm with their father or left with a neighbor in their building. Either way, they were self-sufficient from their early years. Luckily, Irena was mature and responsible at the age of four so she kept the younger sister, who was quite rambunctious, under control. Somehow it all worked out for the best.

The young couple worked hard and saved up as much money as possible to help their children and families in the post-war ravaged villages where they were raised so long ago. Their farm houses and lands now belonged to the Lithuanian's who were dominated by the Soviets. All the local farms were owned by the state and were transformed into communes at the will of the governing Communists. Maria and Jozef lived in hope, recited the Rosary daily, and often fell asleep on a "Hail Mary" bead. They believed with all their hearts that they would see their children soon and all would achieve a better life.

Chapter Fifteen

"Jozef, may I talk to you after Mass today?" asked the Polish organist at St. Isadore's Roman Catholic Church.

"Of course, is something wrong?" he questioned.

"I have information that might please you," was a brief response as the man ran off to begin organizing his music and the choir.

Maria and the children, all dressed in spotless clothes their mother brought from England, looked at Jozef quizzically.

"We'll talk to him after the service," was all he said.

Once Jozef spotted the music director exiting the church, he approached him and the man began speaking to the couple.

"Jozef, I've been observing you and your family this past month and I've heard from Mr. Sawicki that you are an excellent worker and a fine family man. I have a proposition for you. I learned that the Monsignor at a church in Huntington is in need of a custodian for the church and school. He will provide a house for you and your family and pay you $130 a month to work there. Would you be interested if I drove you and your family there to meet him?" asked the organist.

"Of course I'll go with you!" replied Jozef at the

suggestion of a better job opportunity.

" And you said there was a school?" Maria asked the helpful man.

"Yes, next door to the church and your girls would be able to attend," he replied.

"That would be perfect if he agrees to hire us!"

That week the family piled into the generous man's car and he drove them to Huntington. The Right Reverend Monsignor Thomas Murray took a liking to the family and they agreed to arrive at the end of the week and begin working at St. Patrick's Church and the surrounding parish buildings and grounds.

Their home for the next twenty-three years in America was at 22 Anderson Place. The house was a Victorian style home with a front porch, a kitchen, front parlor, living room, dining room, three bedrooms and an indoor bathroom on the second floor. No longer did Maria have to fill up buckets with water, bring it to large pots in the kitchen and then heat it up on the stove in order to bathe her girls in a washtub. Granted there was no heat in the bathroom which made bathing in the winter interesting, but it was all indoors. No more outhouses for this family!

The good priest provided two beds with new mattresses, a table top (to which Jozef made wooden legs) and four kitchen chairs, and most importantly a brand new refrigerator. The day after the family arrived they were visited by the twenty Dominican sisters from the convent adjacent to their new home, along with Sister Monica, the sister in charge of the school and convent. Each nun brought a gift for the family. Sister Stanislaus, or Sister Cookie, as she was called, brought a couple of casseroles, a dish previously unknown to Maria and her family. The other Sisters brought new towels, soaps, toys for the girls, and various articles. Sister Monica brought a sapphire blue children's chair for the girls to share and a white circular plaster wall plate depicting the Child Jesus which she made herself. Verbal communication was nearly impossible; however, sincere hugs for all the Sisters were self-explanatory.

"Jozef, how blessed we are. We survived so much and here we are welcome by these angelic women," uttered the overjoyed Maria.

"Yes, God has continued to help us. And I know we'll succeed in this country even though it won't be easy," he mused.

Jozef plunged into his new job and worked hard to keep the church, school, and grounds in proper shape. He became acclimated quickly to his new role, but at times recalled how he was master of his father's farm in Poland and people worked for his family. Now, he took direction from priests, nuns, teachers, and even a student now and then until the youngster, usually a boy, was reprimanded by a nun. Maria worked in the rectory cleaning and cooking for the priests along with Josephine, an older Italian woman in her sixties who was somehow related to Tomas, an older Italian man who worked alongside Jozef, or Joe, as he was now called. Maria also cleaned homes for well-to-do families in Huntington Bay and Lloyd Harbor when not working in the rectory. She also took in ironing in order to add to the family income. Monies saved were sent to Poland to provide for Helena and Bronia and the rest of the family.

School was not what Jozef was truly interested in attending at the age of forty-four, but he needed to learn English so he began classes at Huntington High School in the evenings. It was very difficult for him to get a grasp of this language, but he tried. Maria also went to classes a few times, but when the teacher asked her to write a sentence on the board she was so embarrassed by her lack of ability, she never returned. She and Jozef continued to sit at the kitchen table and study vocabulary and attempt to read. Eventually, they mastered rudimentary skills and at least could speak to store clerks and neighbors. Once Irena went to kindergarten and learned English, they relied on her to translate for them with doctors, dentists, lawyers, and anyone else with whom they needed to communicate.

"Maria, I just met two Polish men in English class who need a place to live. If I ask Monsignor Murray's permission to rent them the bedrooms upstairs, we could charge ten dollars for the room and board and save more money," stated the excited husband.

And this was how the family first took in two boarders and then three. The men were also displaced Poles in their twenties and thirties who arrived in America from Germany. They were taken from their homes and families in 1940 and sent to Germany where they were slave laborers on farms, in factories, or in the construction of rails, bridges, and roads bombed by the Allies. Because they were young and strong, their fate was not imprisonment in concentration camps but work in slave labor details. Maria cooked and did their laundry which was not easy since she washed all the clothing by hand in the bathtub using a washboard. But as soon as enough money was saved, she bought a washing machine. Maria still had to wring the clothes through a hand turned press, but the machine did all the washing. This was progress! Hanging the clothes on the lines outside was difficult, especially in the winter, but the couple only considered the money they garnered for their family in Poland.

The boarders, Mr. Tadeusz Boczkowski, Mr. Jozef Kaczmarski, Mr. Roman Grochowina, and at one point Mr. Stanislaw Szubka, when Mr. Grochowina moved to Buffalo, occupied the three bedrooms upstairs, while the family of four converted the living room into their sleeping quarters. With time, each of the men found a bride and moved into their own homes, but the friendships formed lasted for a lifetime. Maria and Jozef were like parents to them and even Godparents to their children. This new land and these strangers became family. The last tenant, Mr. Stanislaw Lyczek (Mr. Stanley) remained with the family until 1956 when he also took a bride.

During all this time, Maria and her husband had one goal in mind – citizenship. They studied daily about the United States and its government so that they could get their documents. They quizzed each other and learned to write "I love America," and "The President of the United States is Dwight Eisenhower," and other simple sentences in order to be ready on their appointed day in court. They knew they had to be able to read and write in English and answer questions posed to them about the government. Maria and her husband worked hard to achieve this goal so they could bring their daughters to America once they achieved citizenship.

Bronislawa was twenty years old and unmarried so

she would be able to come first, still being considered a minor. Helena was married and had two sons so this process would take longer. But the couple was determined to be reunited with their family and hired an attorney to help with the paperwork. He was Joseph Plonski, a Polish-American attorney with a practice in Huntington and he worked diligently to unite the family.

Finally, in the Spring of 1957, word arrived that Bronislawa received a visa to exit Poland.

"My God Jozef, I can't believe we will have our daughter here tomorrow. I can't sleep a wink!" said Maria excitedly. She had already prepared a bedroom, purchased all the necessary clothing and toiletries and cooked a feast of Polish foods.

"She was so little, only three and small for her age when we were arrested. I hope she'll be glad to see us and meet her sisters," continued Maria.

Mr. Plonski drove the family to the airport to meet their daughter. As they awaited the arrival of passengers, he said to Maria, "Only seventeen more minutes for the plane to arrive."

"Yes, Mr. Plonski, I think these last seventeen minutes are worse than the last seventeen years!" replied the visibly shaken mother.

As can be imagined, the reunion was a tearfully joyful moment for everyone. Mr. Plonski informed the newspapers about the arrival of this young woman and there were reporters present to photograph the event. Parents and daughter were in a state of shock after not seeing each other for so many years. Actually, Bronislawa, or Bronia as she was called, did not remember her parents since she was so young when they were separated and as future years would show, the parent/child bonding would prove to be a difficult, if not insurmountable, process. But for the moment all were overjoyed.

The following weekend, Maria and Jozef invited all the nuns, priests, and Mr. Plonski to dinner to celebrate the reunion with their daughter. By then, she bought new clothing, made in America, for Bronia along with new shoes and some costume jewelry. Mrs. Dulko, now Mrs. Pilecki, with whom she suffered so much in Soviet Russia and the Middle East, was also present. After the sojourn in England, Mrs. Dulko moved to Argentina along with many widowed and single displaced Poles. There she met Mr. Pilecki, and they married and eventually arrived on Long Island to also settle in Huntington. Mrs. Dulko's children were still in Poland following the war and remained there with their families. Eventually, she visited Poland to reunite with her children and help them financially. Helena's youngest daughter, Maria, from who she was forcibly separated when the child was an infant, came to America with Mr. Plonski's legal help and eventually married and raised her son and daughter in America.

The festivities lasted into the evening with Mr. Plonski and Irena as translators. In the excitement, Mrs. Pilecki forgot to put the gravy on the dinner table until the meal was almost over. She was very apologetic to the guests, but no one cared since the dinner was secondary to the happiness everyone shared with the family.

Bringing Helena, her husband Michal, and their sons Janusz, (John) and Wladyslaw (Walter) to New York would take much longer. First the family had to move from

Michael's hundreds of acres of farmland, which was now a Soviet collective, to Szczecin, Poland. Michael's nephew lived there after the war and could help them procure an apartment. In the United States, the government would only permit Helena to come permanently without her family, and this was unacceptable to her parents.

"Irena, I want you to write a letter to the President explaining our life history and indicating that your father and I are opposed to separating Helena's family after all we went through," stated Maria to her fourteen year old daughter.

Dutifully, Irena wrote as her mother dictated about the necessity for the whole family to immigrate as one unit and be unified with the rest of the family.

Whether the President ever saw the letter, no one knew, but eventually a reply arrived from the Department of Immigration indicating that Helena and her family could reapply for a visa and would not be refused.

The young family arrived in Huntington in 1961, to the thrill of Jozef and Maria. Their family was now complete! Helena being seven when she was torn from her parents' arms, remembered them well. The transition was still difficult for everyone, but all were together.

Maria and Jozef's dream of being reconnected with their children was finally realized and now their children, ten grandchildren, and thirteen great-grandchildren could prosper in their grandparent's newly adopted country.

It is said that God answers prayers in his own time not according to our timetable, and in this case Maria's prayers were answered, albeit after twenty years – but answered.

Afterward

In 1973, Maria and Jozef returned to Poland for a six week visit. It was an opportunity to see their family after thirty-three years. Their brothers and sisters were all married and had grown children and grandchildren. Their parents had long passed which made the trip heartbreaking since they could not stop at their graves to place flowers and pray. Their parents were buried in the churchyard cemeteries of their respective villages outside of Vilnius, Lithuania. Jozef and Maria did not request visas to their old homelands since they did not trust the Soviet government and were fearful of being deported to the Soviet Union again. As Jozef used to say, "I've spent enough time vacationing in Siberia!"

The reunion was wonderful for everyone and all the relatives wanted them to return to Poland permanently, but Maria and Jozef loved America and reaffirmed that they would never return to a country where Communism reigned, as it did in Poland at that time.

Maria and Jozef retired from St. Patrick's Church after twenty-three years and moved to Huntington Station, New York. Jozef died when an aneurysm ruptured near his aorta at the age of seventy-five on May 8, 1982. Maria lived until the age of almost ninety-six and moved on to her maker on January 11, 2010. She was lucid up to one week prior to her death and remembered her family members. She lived to see her children become successful in America along with her grandchildren, and great-grandchildren. Everyone acquired college degrees, which made her immensely proud, and all achieved success in their chosen careers.

The huge, black cross from Maria's dream from so many years ago, which collapsed before her, was prophetic of her life. To the young prisoner it indicated that her horror would end and that her life would stabilize. Though at that time, as she cowered in the many prison cells she occupied, she did not know how or when. In her frail hands, as she was dying, she held her favorite Rosary beads with the crucifix clutched between her fingers. She sincerely believed that her exceptionally strong faith in God and her constant litany of prayers kept her alive throughout her war experiences as it did her husband, Jozef.

Sprawozdanie z przeżyć
na obczyźnie z dniem
aresztowania i opuszczenia
domu rodzinnego.

22. Marca zostałam areszto-
wana. Zamknięta zostałam
z dziećmi w majątku p. Tartaty
W dniu tym samym podczas
wielkiego mrozu wywieźli
mnie z dziećmi i mężem
do Oszmianki. Tam nas
trzymali przez 3 dni.
Po trzech dniach dzieci
odesłali do rodziny męża
ponieważ przyjechali po
nich rodzice męża.
A mnie z mężem odesłali
do więzienia w Oszmian

24. W dniu świąt Wielkanocnych byłam razem z mężem w więzieniu rzerej w ciemnej piwnicy gdzie nie było okien promyk słońca nie dochodził. Bardzo dużo było znajomych jeść nie miałyśmy co dzieliłyśmy się okruchami chleba. W międzyczasie zabrali męża dokąd nie wiadomo. Po tygodniu przewozili nas z tego więzienia do Starej Wilejki w drodze spotkałam się z mężem. Jak również w więzieniu przez trzy miesiące byliśmy razem nie widywałyśmy się z tem tylko że mąż

mnie widział czas do
czasu gdy szłyśmy do
łaźni, a ja jego wcale
nie widziałam.
Po jakimś czasie z tego
więzienia przewieźli do
drugiego. Wsadzili do celi
w której było nas 27 osób
a właściwie miejsca było
na 7 osób spałyśmy na
zmianę gdy jedni spali
drudzy siedzieli. Potrwało
tej męczarni trzy miesiące
Po trzech miesiącach
tego siedzenia wywozili
nas do Rosji do Połocka
tu zobaczyłam przypad
kowo męża w transporcie
lecz z nim nie dali

„porozmawiać",

W Potocku znów dostałam się do więzienia o mężu nie miałam żadnej wiadomości. W więzieniu przesiedziałam z nieznanymi saniami dwa miesiące. W między czasie kazali nam się spakować nie wiadomo dokąd w końca na swój wyrok. Sąd wymierzył nie dużo, bo tylko 5 lat ciężkich robót w lagrach. W kilka dni po wyroku wieźli nas do Rosji. Transport był bardzo duży między ludźmi zobaczyłam męża o którym nawet

nie wiedziałam, że siedzią
obok mnie za ścianą
porozumieliśmy się, że mąż
też dostał 5 lat, a nawet
rozmawiałam z nim
pocieszał mnie, że może
Bóg da, że szczęśliwie
przetrwamy i nasza męczar
ze nie długo się skończy.
Nas powieźli na Północno
Mordowska obł. do lagru
a męża dokąd niewiadom
Pracowałyśmy bardzo ciężko
na ten konstrukci czarn
chleba bo zaledwie 500 gr
i wyczekiwałyśmy jakiegoś
zmiłowania. Po niejakim
czasie przenieśli mnie
na drugi punkt gdzie

kazali mnie szyć o czym
nie miałam pojęcia
w przeciągu pięciu dni
musiałam się nauczyć.
Po niejakimś czasie szycie
zaczęłyśmy robić rękawic
na normę dzienną wypa-
dało zrobić szydełkiem
13 rękawiczek dniami 4½
pracowało się na 400 g chleba
i wody. Chodziłyśmy jak
cienie sukienki się kręciły
na nas. Kto jeszcze dosta-
wał pomoc z rodziny to
jakoś biej ....
W sierpniu wyczytałyśmy
w gazecie, że nareszcie
ten dzień upragniony nad
zawarcia ... układu

z rządem polskim Anglję
i Amerykę z Rosją po nie-
długim czasie nas
zwolnili powiedzieli nas
że jesteśmy wolne nieza-
leżne od nich. każda
mogła jechać gdzie chce
Kazali nam do miasta
jenkirta dali nam po
50 rubli na drogę. Przyjecha
łyśmy do Snuraje...
a z tąd do miasta
Sarańsk.
W Sarańsku byłyśmy 3 d...
wyjścia żadnego nie był
i wróciłyśmy do Snuraje w
gdzie też nie wiedziały...
co mamy robić bez opiek
i chleba i kopiejki.

Spotkałyśmy jednego
Polaka biednego podartego
i on właśnie poradził
nam jechać do Buzułuku,
że tam jest organizacje
polskiego wojska posłucha-
łyśmy i odchodził szlon
jechali mężczyźni do
Buzułuka i przyłączyłyśmy
się do nich. W tym
transporcie zachorowałam
na dezenterię obcy czło-
wiek się mną opieko-
wał ratował mnie którego
nazwiska nieznam.
W Buzułuku wstąpiłam
do wojska warunki życiowe
się poprawiły czułam się
dobrze między swoimi.

Spotkałam znajomego sąsiada
Załeszczurewa którego nie
poznałam jak również Hele Duda
W listopadzie z Burmutuka
wywieźli mnie do Uzbekiestan
koło Taszkientu za rzekę Amu
darję tu miałam towarzyszkę
Hele Dulkowę z którą
przeżywałyśmy wspólne
chwile dobre i złe.
Jadąc za rzekę jechałyśmy
wodą przez 5 dni zawieźli
nas do kołchozu pracowały
śmy tam w polu zbie-
rałyśmy watę na normy.
a warunki takie same
jak na sybirze ludzie
umierali z głodu pano
wały różne epidemie.

zwłaszcza dzieci bardzo
umierały. Miałyśmy szczęście
bo byłyśmy załadowani tylko
tydzień zawieźli nas w drugie
gie miejsce również tą
rzeką jechałyśmy i spowro-
tem do kołchozu.
Warunki były straszne
będąc tu przez 3 miesiące
chleba nie widziałam
dostawałam 400 gr zboża.
W jednej kibitce małej
mieszkało nas 25 osób.
Mieszkałyśmy tu do nie
opisania Spało się jedna
przy drugiej, a blondynki
po nas spacerowały.
Tak spędziłyśmy również
święta Bożego Narodzenia.

Urządziłyśmy wspólnie
skromną kolację w dzień
wigilii nastrój był ponie
borowy, bo zamiast się
cieszyć tośmy płakali
każdy wspominał rodzinę
znajomych i dom swój
myślami błądziłyśmy
tam gdzieś w ojczyźnie
zdawałyśmy sobie spraw
jak ona jest daleko
i kiedy do niej wrócimy
wspominałyśmy rodziców
mężów i dzieci o których
nic nie wiedziałyśmy.
Po trzech miesiącach dowie
działam się, że w Iranie
przyjmują do wojska
z wielką trudnością wyru

Tyśmy się z kołchozu i przy-
jechałyśmy do Guzar
Nim przyzwyczaiłyśmy się
do tego życia trwało to
długo warunki były
straszne było zimno
deszcze padały spałyśmy
w namiotach na ziemi
okryć nic było się czem.
Po komisji umunduro-
wali nas i spotkałam
z Wilna rotmistrza
Nawińskiego który za-
opiekował się swoimi
wilnionkami i przyrzekł
że nas nie opuści.
Pracowałyśmy w kuchni
sztabowej 24 godzin przez
zmian gdzie żywiło się

przeszło 3 tysiące wojska.
W Gurzane panowała straszn.
epidemia ~~panow~~ chorowali
na Tyfus dziennie umiera
40 osób przez pół roku zmar
3 tysiące ludzi wojskowych
jak cywilnych.
21. Marca nastąpił wyjazd
za granicę. ja jednak
pozostałam.
18 Odbyła się przysięga P.SK
do której ja również stawała
W czasie pobytu w Gurzane
odwiedzali nas nasi dowód
Generał Bogusz Szyszko
gen. Anders i biskup. Gawli
Ostatni raz będąc Senerał
Anders przemówił ~~do~~ nas
jak do żołnierzy jak

również oznajmił nam, że
za kilka dni wyjedziemy
za granicę, że kres naszej
męki skończy się było
to dla nas poprostu
szczęściem, o którem tak
marzyłyśmy.
11. Sierpnia załadowali
nas do wagonów i opóści-
łyśmy Józar dolinę śmierci
w której tylu pozostało
Polaków, który już nigdy
nie wrócą.
Przyjechałam szczęśliwie
do Krasnowocka 13 tu
pobyłyśmy 3 dni a wody
nie było czekałyśmy
na transport tysiące ludzi.
Ja zachorowałam zaniesli

mnie na noszach do szpita[

Ze jednak pojechałam raz[

koleżankami.

17. Rano załadowałam się

na okręt jechałyśmy przez

morze Kaspijskie.

19. Przyjechałam do portu

Pachlewi w Iranie. Ponie[

Krampiąc się ~~moru~~ dostać

z tego molari leżałam

przez 2 tygodni w przydzia[

dla malaryczek. brałam tu

się doskonałe warunki by

~~kube~~ bardzo dobre.

Razem z chorymi wyjechał[

do Teheranu do Szpitala

P.C.K. poleżałam tydzie[

zostałam przydzielona do

4-Tego obozu.

— — — przyjechałam
do Kanakinu gdzie długo
nie pobyłam. Zmieniłam
znów m.p. przywieźli
nas do Kizył-Rybat.
W marcu dostałam przydział
do Bagdadu.
W Bagdadzie ciężko zacho-
rowałam byłam na operacji
i skierowali do 3-ciego
szpitala w Kizył-Rybat.
Wielkanocne święta spę-
dziłam w szpitalu. W tym
czasie przed chorobą spo-
tkałam męża od tak
długiego czasu. Będąc
w szpitalu odwiedził mię.
W maju przechodziłam
operację.

Hereruru wróciłam ze
szpitala do Bagdadu
mieszkałam w domu
wypoczynkowym przez 18 dn
Po wypoczynku dostałam
przydział do Kirkuku do
1-nego szpitala.
7. Lipca wyjechałyśmy
z Bagdadu.
8. Rano byłyśmy na nowy
m.p. Kirkuk. Dostałam
przydział w Kasynie Sióstr
W między czasie odwiedz
tam męża jak również
mąż mnie. Po kilku
tygodniach nastąpił
wyjazd do Palestyny.
3. września cały personal
szpitala opóścił Kirkuk

wyjeżdżając do Palestyny.
W Palestynie w obozie
przejściowym odpoczywa-
tyśmy 8-dni. to dnia
przez ten czas odwiedałam
męża. Po odpoczynku
wyjechałyśmy znów do
Egiptu do Kantary
tutaj stał trzy szpital.
Po jakimś czasie otrzy-
małam 2-Tygodniowy
urlop do Palestyny.
Pojechałam do męża
mąż również otrzymał
urlop i tych kilkanaśu
dni spędziłyśmy razem
czyje się jak w siebie
w domu. Po urlopie wróciłam
znów do Egiptu do szpitali.

Teraz oczekuję przyjazdu
męża.

Translated by her daughter,
Irena Pawlukiewicz Rozycki

March 22 (1940), I was arrested. I was locked up with my children on the estate of Mr. Tartaly. Later on this same day, during a terrible freeze, I was taken with my children (Helena – 7 and Bronislawa -3) and husband (Jozef) to Oszmianki. They (Lithuanian soldiers) kept us there for three days. After three days, they sent the children back to my husband's family since my husband's parents came to get them. They sent my husband and me to a prison in Oszmiana.

March 29 – On Easter, I was with my husband in a prison, or actually a dark basement where there were no windows and the rays of the sun could not reach. There were many people we knew and we had no food, but we shared whatever crumbs of bread we had. During this time, they took my husband away but to where I did not know. After a week, they moved us from this prison to another one in Stara Wilejka. On route I found my husband. Later we were in the same jail for three months. We were not together, but every now and then my husband saw me as I walked to the latrines or wash rooms, but I rarely saw him. After a while they moved us to another jail. They put me in a cell where there were 27 people but in reality there was room for only seven persons. We took turns sleeping, that is, while some slept, others sat up. This torture lasted for three months. *After the three months of sitting in this cell, they (Russian soldiers) transported us to Potock in Russia. There, by accident, I saw my husband in the transport, but they would not allow me to speak to him.*

In Potock I was again in jail; I had no information about my husband. I was in prison for many months with women I did not know. In the meantime, we were told to pack our belongings because we were going to be sentenced and sent somewhere, but we did not know where. I did not receive many years, only five, according to the court, of hard labor in a work camp. A few days after the sentencing, we were moved to Orszy. The transport was huge, but in the midst of the crowds I spotted my husband about whose situation I knew nothing. I found out later that he had been in the same prison as I, only in the next cell. We had a brief opportunity to speak to each other and I found out that he was sentenced to five years of hard labor. He tried to cheer me up by saying that, God willing, we would survive this ordeal and our suffering would soon end.

The other women and I were taken by train (cattle car) to a labor camp in Pocma Mardowska. At the camp, we worked very hard for a 500 gram piece of black bread, while we awaited some kind of merciful relief. After a while, I was sent to another area where I was forced to sew, something about which I had no idea, but had to learn within five days. After a while

*of sewing, we began to knit gloves (for the soldiers).
To reach our daily quota and receive 400 grams of
bread and water, we had to knit thirteen gloves. We
walked like shadows – our dresses flowing on our
bodies. Those who received parcels from their families
survived better.*

*In November (1942), I was sent from Buzuluk
to Tashkent in Uzbekistan across the Amu Dar 'Ya
River. Helena Dulko (Pilecki), an old neighbor from
my hometown, was my companion here and we
experienced good and bad situations. We travelled on
the river for five days and were brought to another
labor camp. We worked in the fields picking cotton to
fulfill our quota. The standard of living was the same
as in Siberia – people dying from hunger or various
epidemics. Children succumbed most readily. We were
lucky because we were there only one week when we
were taken across the same river to another labor
camp. The living conditions were horrible and I was
there for three months during which time I never saw
a piece of bread since I received only 400 grams of
grain. Twenty-five persons lived in one small hut. Our
life here was beyond description. We slept one next to
the other as lice walked from one person to the other.
We spent Christmas here. We scrapped together a
meager meal for Christmas Eve but the atmosphere
was that of a funeral. Instead of being happy, we all
wept. Everyone spoke about their families, neighbors*

and homes. Our memories wandered to our homeland which we realized was so far away and we wondered when we would return. We reminisced about our parents, husbands, and children about whom we had no information.

It took a long time to get used to labor camp life. The living conditions were horrible. It was freezing, constantly raining, and we slept in tents on the bare ground with very little to cover our bodies.

In August (1943), we read in a newspaper that at last the long desired day had arrived. An agreement was made between the Polish government in exile, England, America, and Russia. After a brief time, we were released. The guards and camp commanders told us we were free to go where we pleased. They gave us 50 rubles for our journey and said we could go to a city called Jeozkirta. We arrived in a town called Gruzajewsk instead and from there travelled to Saransk.

We were in Saransk for three days, but there was no way out of there so we returned to Gruzajewsk where we also did not know what to do since now we had no bread or money. Here we met a very poor, bedraggled Polish man who suggested that we go to Guzar because there were people who were organizing former prisoners and helping them sign up for the Polish Army. We listened to him and got on a flatbed railcar which was about to leave with many men for

Guzar. Therefore, we went along with them. During the trip on this transport train, I became very ill with dysentery. A man, a stranger to me, and whose name I did not know, took care of me and saved me. After much hardship, I arrived in Guzar.

When I got to Guzar, I joined the Army and my standard of living improved and I felt comfortable among my own people. I encountered a neighbor from my town, Mr. Latyszowicz, whom I did not recognize at first. I also encountered another neighbor, Helena Dulko.

After we passed the medical commission, we were given uniforms. I ran into the Cavlary Captain, Mr. Nowinski, from Wilno, who took care of his townspeople and swore that he would never leave us. We worked in the commissary kitchen in 24 hour shifts where we fed three thousand soldiers. During this time in Guzar, a terrible typhus epidemic manifested itself. Forty people died daily and three thousand soldiers and civilians died in a half year's time.

On the 10th of May, there was a PSK (Polish Volunteer Women's Military) swearing in ceremony in which I participated. During this time in Guzar, we were visited by our military leaders General++ Bohusz-Szyszko, General Anders, and also Bishop Gawlina. General Anders gave a speech to the soldiers and informed us that in a few days we would be moved across the border and that our suffering here would end. This for us was the luck we were so worried about and awaited.

On the 11ᵗʰ of August, we were put on transport trains and we left the Guzar Valley where we left so many deceased Polish people who would never return home again. I arrived in Krasnovodsk safely on the 13ᵗʰ and we stayed here for three days. There was no water as thousands of people awaited the next transport trains. I became ill and was taken on a stretcher to a hospital, but after I recovered I left on the train with my female companions. On August 19ᵗʰ I arrived at the seaport in Pahlavie in Tranie (Persia). We bathed in the Caspian Sea and I became ill with malaria. I was hospitalized in the ward for those with malaria for two weeks. Eventually, I recovered and felt excellent since the quality of life here was very good. Before recovering, I was moved to a hospital in Tehran along with other patients. I was kept in the hospital for one week and then assigned to the 4ᵗʰ military camp. I arrived in Kanagin where I did not remain for long and was moved again, this time to Kizil-Ribot. In March, I was assigned to Baghdad.

While in Baghdad, I became ill and had surgery. I was sent to the Third Army Hospital in Kizil-Ribot. I spent Easter in the hospital. At this time, just before I became ill, I was reunited with my husband after such a long time (two and a half years). He visited me while I was hospitalized. In May I had surgery and after this

I was sent back to Baghdad to a convalescent home where I recuperated for eighteen days. After this rest, I was assigned to the First Army Hospital in Kirkuk. On the 7ᵗʰ of July, I was sent back to Baghdad. On the 8ᵗʰ of July, I moved into my new quarters with the nurses. After a few weeks orders arrived and we were all moved to Palestine. On September 3ʳᵈ all army hospital personnel left Kirkuk for Palestine. In Palestine we had an eight day leave and I used this time to visit my husband. After this rest period, we were sent to Egypt to Qantara where the First Army Hospital was housed. After a while, I was given a two week pass to Palestine. My husband was also granted a leave and we spent the time together. We felt like we were home together. I returned to Egypt to my hospital, where I awaited my husband's next visit.

Note: The women in the Polish Auxiliary Women's Service (PSK) or "Ochotniczki" were asked by their commanding officers to write a short history of their incarceration in the USSR. My mother wrote hers, but I never saw it until a few years before she died when she gave it to me. This brief diary, which is included here, began my research into her experiences and that of my father.

IRENA MARIA ROZYCKI

British 8th Army, Polish 2nd Corps, 3rd Carpathian Rifle Division (Anders Army) – Maria and Jozef's War Medals

Top Row

King George VI War Medal (1939-1945) Lion on the reverse.
King George VI Defense Medal (1939-1945) Lions, Royal
 Crown, and Oak Leaves on the reverse. Presented to
 Jozef for Bomb Disposal Duty.
Italy War Star (1939-1945).
British War Star (1939-1945).
Pope Leo XIII Jerusalem Cross.
Monte Cassino Cross – Awarded to Jozef for participation in
the Battle of Monte Cassino, May, 1944.
Monte Cassino Cross – Awarded to Maria for her service in the
 Military Hospital at Monte Cassino, May, 1944.

Middle Row

Two Military Bars
Pin - 5th Carpathian Rifle Division Badge.
WWII Polish Army Eagle – worn on the cap.
Pin – Cross with the Numeral 3 in the center – Breast Badge
 for the 3 DSK –3rd Carpathian Rifle Division.
Three Military Bars.

Third Row

Spruce Tree Badge – Emblem of the Polish 3rd Carpathian
 Rifle Division.
Cross on Shield Badge – British 8th Army Insignia.
Mermaid Emblem – Polish 2nd Army Corps.
Cross on Shield Badge – British 8th Army Insignia.
Spruce Tree Badge – Emblem of the Polish 3rd Carpathian
 Rifle Division.

Map of Poland partitioned by the Germany and
The Soviet Union

Map of Soviet slave labor camps - WWII

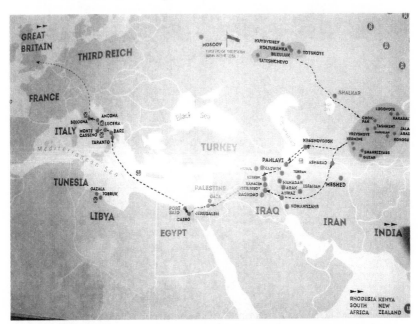

The route of Polish prisoners of war from Siberia to Italy

Maria with two other nurse's aids

Maria and fellow female volunteers in the Polish Army

Maria's army division on parade

Maria and army friends in Baghdad.

General Anders – 1940's

Maria outside the military
camp in the Middle East

Jozef, at approximately age 20, in the Polish Army
(1926-1927)

Maria in military
uniform

Jozef in Palestine in a photo
he sent his daughter, Helena,
in the 1940's

Maria – 1943

161

Jozef, fourth from the left,
receiving a medal

Jozef with a fellow soldier

Jozef with an army friend

Jozef (first from the left) and army friends in Palestine

Jozef (standing second on the left) with his platoon

Jozef outside his tent

163

Religious procession conducted for the Polish Army

Camp for released prisioners from Siberia in Iran

Maria and Jozef's
happy reunion

Photo Jozef sent to Maria expressing his desire to see her
again and about how worried he was about their future

Maria and Jozef 1944-1945

Jozefina and Pawel with their
daughter Bronislawa, son-in-law
and grandson, Czeslaw

Pawel Pawlukiewicz –
Maria's father

Pawel and Stefania Pawlukiewicz, Jozef's parents,
and their grandchild

Pawel and Stefania Pawlukiewicz – Jozef's parents with family
members. Bronislawa (Bronia) is in the center and Helena is
directly behind her (third from the left) in front of the family home

Helena and Bronislawa
Pawlukiewicz after
WWII – c.1950

Helena Pawlukiewicz –
Poland

Bronislawa, Poland, 1959

Helena and her husband, Michal Pawlukojc with their sons,
John and Walter, Poland

Maria Rudzinska (Maria's cousin and a bridesmaid at
her wedding) with her husband, Stanislaw and children,
Leszek, Krystyna and Janusz, Morag, Poland, 1950's

Jan and Jadwiga Pawlukiewicz, Jozef's brother
and his wife, Gierdziejewce, Poland, 1947

Aleksander and Stanislawa Pawlukiewicz, Maria's
brother and his wife, with their children, Halina
and Piotr, Olsztyn, Poland

Stanislaw and Veronika Pawlukiewicz, Maria's oldest brother,
with his wife and children, 1974, Vilnius, Lithuania

Marian and Michalina
Pawlukiewicz, Joseph's
youngest brother and his wife,
Morag, Poland, 1969

Maria and Irena,
Christmas, 1966

Bronislawa and her cousin, Regina, Wilno, 1955

Maria and Irena,
Diddington Hospital,
England, 1947

Mr. Ludwik Szulc, Irena's
Godfather, Diddington,
England, 1947

Teresa's Christening, 1948, England. Forefront : Irena and
Anna Chmara; Seated: Mrs. Helena Dulko, Maria holding
Teresa; Back row: Jozef, Mr. and Mrs. Chmara. Godparents
were Mrs. Dulko and Mr. Chmara

Jozef (standing, second from the right) in a photo sent to
Maria and his daughter, Irena, while recovering in the
military hospital in England, 1947.

Wedding of Jozef's cousin, Viktor Alancewicz to Zofia in England.
Viktor also survived prison camps in Siberia. In the background,
"beczki," Nissen huts where Polish families were housed

Irena and Teresa, England, 1948

Maria and Irena with Polish camp children in Diddington, 1948

Maria, Jozef, Teresa and Irena (in a Polish
"Krakowianka" National Costume) England, 1949.

Irena and Teresa, England, 1949

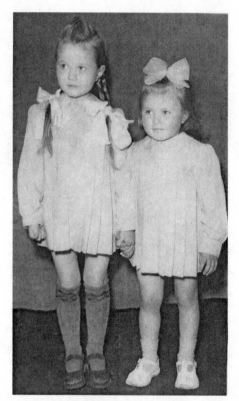

Irena and Teresa just before leaving
for the United States, 1951

Rt. Rev. Msgr. Thomas F.
Murray, who hired Jozef and
Maria to work at St. Patrick's
R.C. Church, Huntington, NY

St. Patrick's R.C. Church, Huntington, NY, 1951

St Patrick's Elementary School, Main Street,
Huntington, NY

Mrs. Sawicki with Irena and Teresa, on
her farm in Aquebogue, NY, 1951

Maria, Jozef , Irena and Teresa in front of their home
on 22 Anderson Place, Huntington, NY, 1950's

Maria and Jozef in front of 22 Anderson
Place, Huntington, NY, 1966

Jozef, Maria, Teresa, and Irena,
Huntington,1960's

Jozef and Maria with Teresa at her
Confirmation, 1959

Bronislawa Pawlukiewicz and her Aunt Stanislawa
Kastanowicz (Maria's youngest sister), 1957, Ploty,Poland

Maria and her daughter after Helena arrived in the
United States, 1962

Maria and Jozef, Huntington,NY, late 1950's

Helena, Bronia, Maria and Irena, Huntington, NY, 1960's

Bronislawa and Walter Kilian with Jozef and Maria,
August, 1957

Helena and Michal Pawlukojc

Teresa and Charles Nauss, 1994

Irena and John Rozycki, 2000

Teresa Pawlukiewicz , graduation from
Huntington High School, NY, 1966

Irena Rozycki,
graduation from
St. John's University,
Jamaica, NY, 1971

Maria's uniform from the Polish Women's
Volunteer Army

Maria and Jozef on their 50th Wedding Anniversary,
September 1, 1980

Sources Consulted

Adamczyk, Wesley. *When God Looked the Other Way: An Odyssey of War, Exile, and Redemption.* Chicago: University of Chicago Press, 2004.

Anders, Wladyslaw (Lt. General). *An Army in Exile: The Story of the Second Polish Corps.* Nashville, TN: Reprinted by The Battery Press, Inc. , 2004.

Burgener, Robert D. *For the Life of a Child: Polish World War II Refugees in Iran.* Iranian.com Archives, November 4, 1997.

Ciczek, Walter J., S.J. *With God in Russia.* Garden City, New York: Imager Books, 1966.

Davies, Norman. *Heart of Europe: The Past in Poland's Present.* New York: Oxford University Press, 2001.

Davies, Norman. *God's Playground: A History of Poland. 2 vols.* New York: Columbia University Press, 1984.

Davies, Norman. *Trail of Hope: The Anders Army, An Odyssey Across Three Continents.* Great Britain: Osprey Publishing, 2015.

Fink-Whitman, Rhonda. *94 Maidens.* Indianapolis, IN: Dog Ear Publishing, 2012.

Frankl, Viktor E. *Man's Search for Meaning.* Boston: Beacon Press, 1959.

Gessner, Peter K. and Wanda Slawinska. *The Siberic Gehenna: The Travails of the Poplewski Family.* The University of Buffalo. http://info-poland.buffalo.edu/classroom/sibir/travails.html.

Goj, Jozef. *NO. 6 Polish General Hospital 1947.* www.TweedsmuirMilitaryCamp.Co.UK.

Gradosielska, Danuta. *My Life in Exile 1939-1946.* http://www.Kresy.co.uk/memories.html.

Hergt, Klaus. *Exiled to Siberia: A Polish Child's World War II Journey.* Cheboygan, Michigan: Crescent Lake Publishing, 2000.

Johnson, Thomas H.,ed. *The Complete Poems of Emily Dickenson.* New York: Little Brown,1961.

Jolluck, Katherine R. *Exile and Identity: Polish Women in the Soviet Union During World War II.*Pittsburgh, PA: University of Pittsburgh Press, 2002.

Jopek, Krysia. *Maps and Shadows.* Los Angeles, CA: Aquila Polonica Ltd., 2010.

Krolikiowski, Lucjan, OFM Conv. *Stolen Childhood: A Saga of Polish War Children.* Buffalo, New York: Fr. Justyn Rosary Hour, 1983. (New edition: San Jose: Authors Choice, 2001).

Krupa, Michael. *Shallow Graves in Siberia.* New Britain, CT: Minerva Press, 1995.

Koskodan, Kenneth K. *No Greater Ally: The Untold Story of Poland's Forces in World War II.* Oxford, UK: Osprey Press, 2009.

Kusmierczak, Michal. " Droga Przez Pieklo, Historia Jana Holko." ("The Road through Hell, The History of Jan Holko.") Wsrod Przyjaciol (Amongst Friends) Magazine. October – November, 1996.

Langer, Rulka. *The Mermaid and the Messerschmitt: War Through a Woman's Eyes 1939-1940.* 2nd ed. East Sussex, Great Britain: Aquila Polonica Limited, 2010.

Mikosz-Hintzke, Teresa. *Six Years 'til Spring: A Polish Family's Odyssey.* New York: Authors Choice Press, 2001.

Parker, Matthew. *Monte Cassino: The Hardest-Fought Battle of World War II.* New York: Anchor Books, 2003.

Pawlukiewicz, Maria. Diary. *Trans. Irena Rozycki. "An Account of My Experiences in Foreign Lands from the Day of My Arrest and the Abandonment of My Family Home."*

Piotowski, Prof. Tadeusz. "Lecture on Deportation and Amnesty." Published in a Polish - Canadian magazine, *Miedzy Nami,* May, 2000.

Pogonowski, Iwo Cyprian, Prof. " *The Truth about Jedwabne and Heroic Deeds of the Polish Nation in The 20th Century."* http://www.iyp.org/polish/history/antypolonizm/jedwabne_en_124. html

Pomykalski, Wanda E. *The Horror Trains: A Polish Woman Veteran's Memoir of World War II.* http://www.polishlibrary.org/review/horror-trains.htm.

Ptasnik, Zofia Ludwika Malachowska. *A Polish Woman's Daily Struggle to Survive: Her Diary of Deportation, Forced Labor, and Death in Kazakhstan: April 13, 1939-May 26, 1941.* http://www.ruf.rice.edu/~sarmatia/102/221ptas.html.

Rising, David, Randy Herschaft, and Monika Scislowska. "Commander of Nazi-led Unit Lives in the United States." Myrtle Beach, SC: *The Sun News,* June 16, 2013.

Rummel, R. J. *from Statistics of Poland's Democide: Addenda.* http://www.hawaii.edu/powerskills/SOD. Chap.7. Addenda. Html.

Sepetys, Ruta. *Between Shades of Gray.* Toronto, Ontario, Canada: Penguin Group Inc., 2011.

Shifrin, Avraham. *The First Guidebook to Prisons and Concentration Camps of the Soviet Union.* New York : Bantam Books, 1982.

Stankiewicz, Sister Christine Marie. *Eugenia Lipinska Stankiewicz's Story.* http://www.anndee.com/tina/mom-story.htm.

Tomaszewski, Irene. Ed. Trans. *I am First a Human Being: The Prison Letters of Krystyna Wituska,* Montreal, Canada: Vehicule Press, 2003.

Topolski, Aleksander. *Without Vodka: Adventures in Wartime Russia.* South Royalton, VT: Steerforth, 2001.

Tuma, Debbie and Jane H. Furse. "Holocaust Baby Gets to Watch Family's Story as Off-Broadway Drama." *NY Daily News,* 2008.

Wood, E. Thomas and Stanislaw M. Jankowski. *Karski: How One Man Tried to Stop the Holocaust.* New York: John Wiley and Sons, Inc. 1994.

Wright, Michael, ed. *The World at Arms, The Reader's Digest Illustrated History of World War II* . London, The Reader's Digest Association, Ltd., 1989.

Wrobel, Piotr. "The Devil's Playground: Poland in World War

II." The Canadian Foundation for Polish Studies of the Polish Institute of Arts and Sciences. Price-Patterson Ltd., 2009.

Novels

Ackerman, Diane. *The Zookeeper's Wife*. New York: W. W. Norton and Company, Inc., 2007.

Benioff, David. *City of Thieves*. New York: Penguin Group, 2008.

Boyne, John. *The Boy in the Stripped Pajamas*. New York: David Fickling Books, 2006.

Busch, Frederick. *A Memory of War*. New York: W. W. Norton and Company, Inc., 2003.

deRosnay, Tatiana. *Sarah's Key*. New York: St. Martin's Griffin Press, 2007.

Grossman, Vasily. *Life and Fate*. New York: The New York Review of Books, 1985.

Hannah, Kristin. *The Nightingale*. Thorndike, Maine: St. Martin's Press, 2015.

Lowry, Lois. *Number of Stars*. New York: Houghton Mifflin Harcourt Publishing Company, 1989.

Mac Innes, Helen. *While Still We Live*. New York: Fawcett, 1985.

Nemirovsky, Irene. *Suite Francaise*. New York: Vintage Books, 2004.

Roy, Jennifer. *Yellow Star*. Las Vegas, NV: Amazon Publishing, 1967.

Shaw, Irwin. *The Young Lions*. Chicago: University of Chicago Press, 1948.

Shreve, Anita. *Resistance*. Boston: Little, Brown and Company, 1995.

Simonov, Konstantin. *The Living and the Dead*. New York: Doubleday and Company, 1962.

Solzhenitsyn, Aleksandr. *One Day in the Life of Ivan Denisovich*. New York: Signet Classic, 1962.

Wiesel, Elie. *Night.* New York: Hill and Wang, 1972.

Wolf, Joan M. *Someone Named Eva.* New York: Clarion Books, 2007.

Yolen, Jane. *The Devil's Arithmetic.* New York: Viking Penguin, Inc. 1988.

Zusak, Markus. *The Book Thief.* New York: Alfred A. Knopf. 2005.

Films

" A Forgotten Odyssey." VHS. London, Great Britain: Lest We Forget Productions. http://www.aforgottenodyssey.com

" In Darkness." Film. Agnieszka Holland, Director. Sony Picture Classics, 2011.

"The Soviet Ethnic Cleansing Campaign Against the Poles during World War II." Http://www.videofact.com/english/samples/E_2/E19_part 2.html.

PAWLUKIEWICZ FAMILY

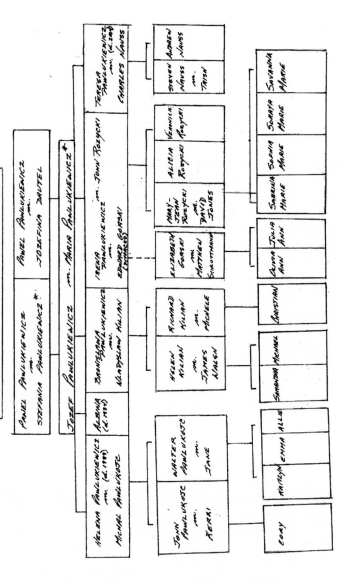

PANEL PAWLUKIEWICZ
m.
JOZEFINA DAUTEL

PAWEL PAWLUKIEWICZ *
m.
STEFANIA PAWLUKIEWICZ *

JOZEF PAWLUKIEWICZ   m. MARIA PAWLUKIEWICZ *

HELENA PAWLUKIEWICZ (d. 1999) m.
MICHAL PAWLUKOTC

ALBINA (d. 1954)

BRONISLAWA PAWLUKIEWICZ m.
WLADYSLAW KILIAN

IRENIA PAWLUKIEWICZ m.
EDWARD GORSKI (DIVORCED)

JOHN ROZYCKI m.

TERESA PAWLUKIEWICZ (d. 2009) m.
CHARLES NAUSS

JOHN PAWLUKOTC m. KERRI

WALTER PAWLUKOTC m. JANE

HELEN KILIAN m. JAMES WALSH

RICHARD KILIAN m. MICHELE

ELIZABETH GORSKI m. MATTHEW SCHATTMANN

MARY-JEAN ROZYCKI m. DAVID JONES

ALICIA ROZYCKI

VERONICA ROZYCKI

STEVEN NAUSS m. TRISH

ANDREW NAUSS

CODY

MADYLYNN EMMA ALLIE

SAMANTHA MICHAEL

CHRISTIAN

OLIVIA ANN

JULIA ANN

SABRINA MARIE

SOPHIA MARIE

SORAYA MARIE

SAVANNA MARIE

* Note: Stefania and Marie had the same maiden name as their married name.

CPSIA information can be obtained
at www.ICGtesting.com
Printed in the USA
FFOW02n1416030718
47258860-50149FF